# CHURCH-FREE SPIRITUALITY:

## How to Craft a Spiritual Practice Beyond the Bounds of Religion

Lightwalker Press

Lee's Summit, MO

Library of Congress Control Number: 2016918859
ISBN: 978-0-9983553-0-6 (for print version)
ISBN: 978-0-9983553-1-3 (for e-book)

Book Design by Ben Jamison and Baz Here
Cover Art and Design by Paul Emerson
Edited by Sharon Lineker

# Table of Contents

# Part 1

# Setting The Stage

If you are reading this book, it is likely because on some level you have an innate knowing that there is more to life than what you have been experiencing. Perhaps it's an unsettled feeling, an eagerness to break free from the monotony of your typical routine. However this experience shows up for you, something within is calling you to deeper, richer, more fulfilling experiences. The urge is there, but how do you go about fulfilling that urge?

Perhaps part of you thinks a church might hold the answer, but the idea of religion just doesn't sit right. Maybe you already are a member of a church but the Sunday services aren't quite doing it for you. There are lots of people who say they are "spiritual but not religious," but what does that really mean? This can all feel very frustrating, especially when you know, internally, that there is more to be had from life!

I know the feeling. I have been there. Following that inner urge, I discovered a new way of looking at life, a new way of being. I found a teacher who helped lead me back to myself through an active practice of spirituality. This practice does not require a church, a religion, blind acceptance of dogma, self-deprecation, or even a teacher or guru. Over the past decade, my dedicated spiritual study and practice has led me to a professional license as a spiritual counselor, a Master's degree in Spiritual Psychology, and a life that is far more rich and fulfilling than I used to think possible.

This book takes all of those years of learning and practice and distills them down to the basics. Nine foundational spiritual practices will be presented along with easy suggestions on how to begin exploring and establishing your own spiritual practice – one that works for you because it is created by you. If you are feeling that pull to "something greater" (or are just curious about spirituality) *Church-Free Spirituality* holds the best tools I have found to help you discover that which you are seeking.

These first six chapters are dedicated to setting the stage for crafting your own spiritual practice beyond the bounds of religion. In the following pages you will discover some of the reasons why establishing a spiritual practice is so vitally important, get some new and empowering definitions of common religious terms, and begin to explore some foundational ideas that must be in place before crafting the practice can begin.

## The Beginner's Mind

Whether you are reading from the perspective of just dipping your toe into the idea of spirituality, or have been studying it for years, I highly encourage you to read this entire book with an open mind - the *beginner's mind*.

The beginner's mind is open and eager to explore. It does not take what it is told as gospel truth, but rather explores what it is given and tries it out to see what happens. The beginner's mind doesn't skip sections of a book, thinking that it already knows. It devours every sentence and every word looking for the new idea that just might change everything. For those of you with any amount of spiritual learning already under your belt, coming at this book with the beginner's mind might be a challenge. However, I invite you to set the intention to do so.

# Chapter One

## Laying The Foundation

The title of this book, *Church-Free Spirituality*, is not intended to imply that church-based spirituality is bad or wrong in any way. I believe that at the heart of every religion or spiritual philosophy is the intention to benefit those who participate with it. Nothing in this book should be construed as religion or church bashing. What works for one person may not work for others. This book simply gives an alternative approach for those people who feel "church" doesn't work for them.

It's never a wise idea to mix religion or spirituality and politics, yet it might be very easy to relate some of the terminology used in this book to political viewpoints. No word used in this book should be assumed or read as to relate to any political party, philosophy, or point of view. For example, any use of the word "liberal" has nothing to with politics but rather relates to (from www.thefreedictonary.com)

> A.  Not limited to or by established, traditional, orthodox, or authoritarian attitudes, views, or dogmas; free from bigotry.
> B.  ...open to new ideas for progress, and tolerant of the ideas and behavior of others; broad-minded.

There may be other words of a similar nature in this book.

*Church-Free Spirituality* is based on the ideas of New Thought and Metaphysics. Though often linked to religion, New Thought and Metaphysics (generally used interchangeably) are more life philosophies rather than religions. The term "metaphysics" comes from ancient Greece. *Metaphysics* was the title of one of the principle works of Aristotle. Through time and translation, the word metaphysics came to mean, roughly, the science of what is beyond the physical. The physical world is viewed in this context as an effect rather than a cause unto itself. Everything you experience on the visible or physical side of life is the result of the invisible or metaphysical side of life.

The easiest example of this is an inventor. An inventor first creates the idea of his or her invention. It exists only as thought, in mind. This thought is invisible to the physical world. It is metaphysical in that it must exist before the physical expression can be produced. After the idea is generated, the inventor then produces a physical prototype: first the thought, then the thing. This holds true in much subtler ways as well. Imagine two people standing next to each other, watching the sunset at the Grand Canyon. One of these people has an incredibly moving experience of the beauty of nature, while the other gets upset that there is no cell service in the area. As silly as that might sound, the truth is that our thought directly affects our experience. New Thought and Metaphysics focus on inner reality, the changing of which dramatically alters outer experience.

Related to this is the term manifestation, which is often used in New Thought and Metaphysics and will be used throughout this book as well. Simply put, manifestation is the process of thoughts becoming things, or the invisible becoming visible. It means bringing something you desire into your experience. Manifestation can relate to physical objects, jobs, relationships, awareness, or a state of being.

## New Thought, Ancient Wisdom

Don't let the word "new" in New Thought throw you. Often times, students of New Thought philosophy follow up the term with the words "ancient wisdom." The only thing new about New Thought is how it's presented and its resurgence into our modern day society. New Thought is the synthesis of the teachings of the saints, sages, mystics, and masters throughout time, put in modern language so you can apply those concepts in your life. New Thought honors all traditions as it recognizes that the heart of all religions and spiritual philosophies are all the same. Just as different languages say the same word differently, different religions attempt to convey the same basic ideas. This truth is easily lost, unfortunately, considering that in addition to translating the teachings through language, they must also be filtered through the cultures that birthed them and the historical environments through which they came.

## You

There is just one more thing that needs to be addressed to "lay the foundation," and that is you. I believe that you are amazing. I believe that you have within you more grace, beauty, glory, and power than you realize. I believe that you can access all of who you truly are, and with it make your life and this planet significantly better. I thank you for your willingness to do so.

Chapter Two

## Why Establish a Spiritual Practice?

*N*othing has a greater ability to positively impact the experience you have on a daily basis than a strong and consistent spiritual practice, or the application of tools and techniques intended to bring you a deeper understanding of your true nature as Spirit. If money were the answer, there would be no depressed millionaires, but there are. If fame were the answer, then no celebrity would ever commit suicide, yet they do.

We live in a spiritual universe. Through quantum physics, science is beginning to prove what the mystics have long said. We are not human beings having a physical experience; we are spiritual beings having a human experience. The invisible or spiritual aspect of us exists before the physical and is superior to the physical. From this perspective, it becomes clear that turning to anything in the physical world, like money, success, or fame, will do little to uplift your experience. Since your true nature is spiritual, the spiritual is where you must focus to have the most powerful, dramatic, and lasting impact.

We all imagine living a different life than we currently do. It might be a better relationship, more friends, more money, a different job, better health, etc. that call to us. Yet there is a tendency that, no matter how good life gets, there is something nagging in the background for "more." What many people don't realize is that the "more" that is craved is not more money, power or friends. The "more" yearned for is more of ourselves, to be in touch with our true spiritual nature as a direct experience.

Humanity yearns to fulfill the ancient Greek aphorism, "Know Thyself." When you arrive at the place where you truly know your Self, through not only logical reasoning, theory, and concept, but also direct experience, then the amount of money you have or the notoriety attached to your name or anything of the physical world will have lost all of its power to negatively impact your experience. The question then becomes, "How do I explore my true nature and have a direct experience?" The answer is through spiritual practice.

The truth is, no matter what you currently think you know about who you are, you are far greater. We all have the ability to be happy, to experience joy, to share love and to live in a constant state of gratitude. We have the power within us to dissolve all perceived barriers and be completely connected with all of Life, exuberantly experiencing the wonder and beauty of creation. Feel into these last several statements. Read them again in the first person.

> *I am far greater than I realize. I have the ability to be happy, to experience joy, to share love and to live in a constant state of gratitude. I have the power within me to dissolve all perceived barriers and be completely connected with all of Life, exuberantly experiencing the wonder and beauty of creation.*

Does a place, deep inside you, whisper "YES!"? Does part of your being resonate and feel aligned with those statements, recognizing them as true? If so, then you have your reason for why to establish a spiritual practice.

If you don't feel the resonance at first, that's okay. Try again. Explore deeper inside. There may be layers of past experience and conditioning in the way. Whether or not you feel an internal resonance with these statements, from a logical standpoint they provide a very compelling reason to establish a spiritual practice.

## The Goal of Spiritual Practice

Ernest Holmes, the founder of Centers for Spiritual Living (formerly Science of Mind or Religious Science) wrote in the organization's statement of beliefs, "I believe the ultimate goal of life to be a complete emancipation from all discord of every nature, and that this goal is sure to be attained by all." The goal of a spiritual practice is the same; complete emancipation from all discord of every nature. In other words, a deep and abiding sense of peace.

Imagine being perfectly at peace, no matter how heavy the traffic. Imagine if nothing anybody said to you would decrease your joy one bit. Imagine that you could stand in the face of someone screaming at you in anger and only have that increase your experience of love for that person. Imagine knowing and feeling that there is always more than enough and therefore nothing to worry about. Now imagine that, as good as imagining all of this feels, you have not even begun to scratch the surface of what this experience might actually be like. These imaginings are the ultimate goal of life and of a spiritual practice. And this experience is attainable.

Of course, this experience will likely not come all at once, but take a great deal of time, effort, attention, intention, energy, and practice. However, progress toward this goal, incremental though it may sometimes seem, has the potential to happen quickly. Given the unfathomable joy of the ultimate goal, even a little progress on the path toward it can have a measurable impact on your experience.

To be sure, few people living on the planet today have come close to attaining this goal, but many are making progress toward it. The more people who participate in a spiritual practice, the more powerful all spiritual practices become, just as more people walking down a path through the forest make that path easier to follow.

## Your Unique Spiritual Path

Everybody's spiritual path and practice is uniquely their own. While many paths are similar, what works for one person doesn't necessarily work for another. There is no right or wrong way to establish a spiritual practice.

> *"You have your way. I have my way. As for the right way, the correct way, and the only way, it does not exist."*
>
> ~Friedrich Nietzsche

Many spiritual paths are similar and complementary. Many are so similar that they can be walked together. Some are so different they come at the practice of spirituality from completely different directions. For this reason, it is wise to not compare your practice or progress to that of anybody else. I will give many examples in this book from my own experience of spirituality. You may have similar experiences, you may not. You have your way. I have my way. My intention is that my way can help you along yours, just as others have helped me along mine.

## My Spiritual Practice

My own spiritual practice began in earnest roughly a decade ago. This commitment to my own spiritual exploration has led me to a license as a spiritual counselor, a Master's degree in spiritual psychology, and a writing and speaking career through which I teach spiritual practices and help others to change their lives. My life today is focused on and centered in spirituality. But, there was a time when I wanted nothing to do with spirituality at all.

I was raised in a family that valued spiritual practice. Instead of attending a typical church, we attended services that were more geared toward a spiritual life philosophy than a religion. As a small boy it was easy. I was surrounded by people who believed in the same ideas, but as I grew older and got out more into the world, I found that most people had a very different idea about religion and spirituality. Moreover, some of those people told me that I was bad because I didn't believe what they did. I saw those ideas being used as an excuse for people to be mean, toward me and toward whole groups of people they had never met. I became so frustrated and disillusioned that I turned away from everything having to do with religion or spirituality.

I was angry. I was hurt. It all seemed so simple and clear to me, yet the world was showing me a very different face. I could point to a teaching that very clearly encouraged loving, only to have somebody else point to a different teaching as a justification of discrimination. I was confused and sick and tired of the contradictions. I was sick and tired of trying to convince others of my point of view. I was sick and tired of defending myself. I decided it would be easier to "throw the baby out with the bath water" and have nothing to do with religion or spirituality ever again!

13

The further I turned from my spiritual practice, the more difficult life became. Rather than choosing what I wanted in life and confidently going after it, I believed myself to be a victim of life's circumstances. I lived in constant fear and felt hopeless and unlovable. Eventually, after years of struggle in a life that wasn't working and was getting worse, I was pushed by pain back to my spiritual roots to "fix my life."

As it turned out, walking distance from where I lived at the time was SpiritWorks Center for Spiritual Living, a spiritual center much like the one I had attended as a child. I walked through the doors the first time, hoping and afraid.

The service was nice, but I was too down on myself to reach out to anybody. I hoped somebody would say hello to me, but nobody did. Then, as I was about to leave, having decided that I was in the wrong place, I made eye contact with one last person... who introduced herself. We talked for a few minutes and a weight lifted from me. There was somebody at SpiritWorks I could talk to, somebody who recognized my silent call for help and answered, somebody my age with whom I had things in common. I could come back to SpiritWorks, I decided.

I did go back, again and again and again. I was a sponge, absorbing everything I could. When classes were offered, I signed up. My life was getting better and the more I learned and practiced what I was learning, the better my life became. Today I live a life that is very different from what it was when I first walked into SpiritWorks. While I am certainly nowhere close to being emancipated from all discord (or upset) of every nature, I have traveled light-years from where I once was.

14

While contemplating this recently, I asked myself, "What if I hadn't found a spiritual center where I could learn about how to establish a spiritual practice? Where would I have gone? What would I have done? Certainly not everybody lives close to a spiritual center, and even if they do, what if it doesn't resonate with them?" That is the reason for this book.

I write this book for the "me" that I was ten years ago. I write this book for people who are frustrated with their religion and want a deeper experience than they think their church can give them. I write this book for people who have never been called to go to church at all, yet recognize that there is more to life than what they see before them. I write this book for you. No matter who you are or where you are on your spiritual journey, if this book is in your hands, it was written for you. I can assure you, based on personal experience, if you apply what this book suggests, your life will get better, and no matter how good it gets it will continue to improve as long as you maintain your spiritual practice.

## Spiritual Practice Is a Practice

Through establishing and maintaining a spiritual practice, life will improve. Over time, you will experience more joy, gratitude, love, abundance, beauty, and excitement. You will feel more connected to Life. You will come to know at a deeper and more powerful level the glory of you. Yet, this will not come without a certain amount of work.

Your spiritual practice will bring things up that must be dealt with. Some things may be obvious. In my story, the belief that I was unlovable was pretty clearly at work in my experience and needed to be addressed. It was no surprise to me when I started my spiritual work that I would be addressing that idea. Other beliefs may be buried so deeply in your subconscious that you have no idea they are even there. Those things will eventually surface and must be addressed.

This is a normal part of the process when making any change in life. The intended change will bring forward all of the beliefs that have previously prevented you from making the desired change. It can be difficult work, but it can also be fun. As you do this work you will find yourself more liberated and experiencing greater joy. There is no work more important and it is doable. The spiritual practices that will be discussed in Part II will help you to work through whatever comes up, the little things and the big things.

A spiritual practice is just that, a practice. When picking up a new hobby, say tennis, you must begin right where you are. It would be very easy to watch Wimbledon and compare yourself to the best in the world, but doing so could easily hinder your growth, if not kick you out of the game all together. On the flip side, without knowing what a professional game of tennis looks like, the goal will be murky and progress will be stunted. The same can be said for a spiritual practice.

Much of the discussion about spiritual practices in this book will include examples that are closer to the ideal than where you may find yourself in the beginning. Don't let this discourage you. Start right where you are. If you try out one of these practices and fail miserably, great! Try it again, and again, and again. How much training does it take to hit a 100-mile-per-hour serve AND hit it accurately? If you tried once and didn't do it, would you quit? If so, you would never hit that serve.

Start with these spiritual practices from right where you are, no matter where that is. It's okay, in fact it's perfect.

It is the only place you can start. As you practice more and more, the practice will become easier and deepen.

Beginning is the key. Decide and commit to establishing a spiritual practice from right where you are and amazing things will happen.

> *"Until one is committed, there is hesitancy, the chance to draw back, always ineffectiveness. Concerning all acts of initiative (and creation), there is one elementary truth, the ignorance of which kills countless ideas and splendid plans: that the moment one definitely commits oneself, the providence moves too. A whole stream of events issues from the decision, raising in one's favor all manner of unforeseen incidents, meetings and material assistance, which no man could have dreamt would have come his way.*
> *I learned a deep respect for one of Goethe's couplets:*
> *Whatever you can do or dream you can, begin it.*
> *Boldness has genius, power and magic in it!"*
>
> ~W. H. Murray

## Spiritual Practice Is Cyclical

Spirituality and spiritual growth is often described as an upward, forward, progressive spiral. As we progress we move up on the spiral, eventually arriving back where we started, but at a higher level.

Let's use a good relationship as an example. A relationship begins when one person asks another on a date. Asking for the second date is easier because of the foundation established by the first date. After a while there is the asking for the relationship to become exclusive. From there one person asks the other to get married. The relationship keeps on coming back to a point where asking and a new beginning is involved, but the asking is at a new, higher level based on the upward, forward progression of the relationship.

> *"We shall not cease from exploration*
> *And the end of all our exploring*
> *Will be to arrive where we started*
> *And know the place for the first time."*
>
> ~T.S. Eliot

We are constantly exploring, returning to where we began and recognizing that place from a new level of experience and growth, and then exploring again. Your spiritual practice will be like this. You will begin a practice, meditation for example, and master it at a certain level only to discover after a time that you are beginning your practice anew but from a depth of experience far beyond where you initially started. Another excellent example of the cyclical nature of a spiritual practice is the Five Stages of the Spiritual Seeker.

Chapter Three

# The Five Stages of the Spiritual Seeker

To a certain extent, we all go though some variation of the spiritual seeker experience. Examining the general unfoldment of this experience can be very helpful in avoiding some of its pitfalls. By recognizing where you are in this process, you can speed your progression through it. In general, this process has five stages:

1. The status quo,
2. Recognizing the status quo isn't working,
3. Releasing the status quo,
4. The Spiritual Seeker, and
5. Arriving at a new status quo.

This process is cyclical and will repeat itself over and over again. This is not a bad thing at all, though at times it may feel like it. Each revolution through the process returns you to the beginning again, yet up-leveled in some way.

The more times somebody goes through the cycle, the less disruptive it tends to become. The more aware you are of the cycle and the more you directly participate with it, the faster you will come through it. Eventually, this process will become not something that happens to you, but rather something you do for yourself, in conscious participation with your spiritual growth.

Keep in mind, your experience may be very different or it might seem like I'm telling your story. What matters most is the awareness you bring to wherever you are in this cycle and that you are okay with being there. Resistance will not stop the cycle; it will just make progress more difficult. Acceptance and participation will speed you along on your way.

**Stage 1 – The Status Quo:**

The status quo simply means things as they are. Wherever a person is on their spiritual journey, so long as they are content with it, they are participating in Stage 1. This stage may last for a very, very long time, be over quite quickly, or anything in between.

**Stage 2 – Recognizing the Status Quo Isn't Working:**

This stage may be something you choose or something that feels forced upon you by circumstances. The more times you have come through the cycle, the more likely it is that this step in the process will be chosen, but nothing is guaranteed.

The amount of time you spend in this stage is directly related to how attached you are to the status quo. If you are very attached to what you used to enjoy and are unwilling to let it go, this stage may last a while, and the longer it lasts the more painful or disruptive it can become.

It may be due to fear that somebody is unwilling to let the status quo go. You may not know what to replace it with, or the fear might be about being adrift. You might have so identified with the status quo, or "given up" so much to get there, that releasing it seems like failure.

Once again, mindset is very important here. If you are willing to recognize the possibility of growth through this process, releasing the status quo will not be seen as a failure but rather a victory!

**Stage 3 – Releasing the Status Quo:**

Eventually, the status quo must be released for growth to take place. As before, mindset and awareness of the process are very important. The more aware you are of what is going on and the more willing you are to participate with the process, the easier and less disruptive Stage 3 can be. Releasing the status quo through conscious choice, while anticipating the newness on the other side of Stage 3, brings ease and grace to the process.

If you are unwilling to release the status quo consciously, it will eventually be released for you. From the inside of such an experience, this can be very painful. It can feel like rejection or having something taken away. In reality though, whether easy or painful, Stage 3 is ultimately in service to your growth.

Keep in mind, and this is exceptionally important, from a spiritual perspective every experience contains within it all that is needed for exceptional growth. When engaging in a spiritual practice, having the willingness to take every experience as being intended for your benefit is vital. No matter how painful or pleasurable, no matter just or unjust, every single experience can be for learning, or it can be concrete shoes pulling you down to the depths. Which the experience becomes is 100% your choice.

**Stage 4 – The Spiritual Seeker:**

In this stage of the cycle you begin to seek for something new; new tools, communities, ideas. Your search is with the intention for growth. You have come through an interesting and potentially intense process of recognizing and releasing what is no longer working in your life and it's now time for that which was not working to be repaired, replaced, or up-leveled.

Given that you are reading this book, it is very likely that you are in this stage. The stage of the Spiritual Seeker can be one of excitement and exploration or one of feeling lost and adrift. Your experience of the stage depends completely upon how you choose to view it.

Your experience is your choice. As you progress you will discover more and more that your true power lies in your power of choice.

The best way to approach this stage in the process is with excitement and curiosity. You are about to discover the next step on your spiritual journey! How exciting is that?! In this stage you get to explore new ideas, try out new spiritual practices, read new authors, the list goes on and on. Perhaps you will discover a slight tweak to an idea that opens up a whole new vista of experience. Perhaps you will be called to create something new.

## Stage 5 – Arriving at the New Status Quo:

Through your explorations in Stage 4, you will have discovered something new in answer to what was no longer working in your life. This new thing shows promise. You like the way it feels and think it might be the answer you were looking for. You follow that feeling and incorporate this new thing into your life as part of the new status quo.

There will be a feeling of newness, which can be exciting and uncomfortable at the same time. The uncomfortableness will subside over time, as it typically does when beginning anything new. Keeping your focus on the excitement will help to dissipate any uncomfortable feelings quicker.

As with all five stages in this cycle, this new status quo may last for years or days. The good news from this stage is that, for now, things have stabilized. The even better news is that at some point in the future, they will shake up again and you will get to incorporate something new and even better into your life. The evolution of your life is always an upward, forward, progressive spiral. Similar issues will surface again and again, but at higher levels.

Eventually, the process of the spiritual seeker becomes as simple as:

- Involved in a fulfilling spiritual practice
- Recognition that the spiritual practice can be tweaked to be more effective
- Opening to new practices or releasing practices that are no longer serving
- Experimenting with adjustments
- Involved in a fulfilling spiritual practice

## Fred's Story: An Example of the Five Stages

My friend, referred to here as "Fred," had found a church that was perfect for him. He had moved his family several states away to become a member of this church and was completely spiritually fulfilled from his membership in and participation with this church. Everything was working well. Fred was in Stage 1 - the status quo.

After a while of participating in this church, Fred began to ask some questions about some of the inconsistencies he was seeing in the behavior of his fellow congregants, as related to the teachings of the church. The church talked a lot about love, for example, but the way outsiders were being treated didn't fit with Fred's growing understanding of love. Rumors about Fred, completely unfounded, began to circulate throughout the community. The community started treating Fred differently and, try as he might, he could not get things resolved. This is Stage 2 – realizing the status quo is no longer working.

The realization that the status quo is no longer working brings Stage 3 – releasing the status quo. For Fred, releasing the status quo did not come easily. Fred had given a lot to join his church. He tried and tried to quell the rumors. He did everything he could to meet with the church leaders to address what was going on, but to no avail. Eventually, Fred and his family were kicked out of the church.

⤳

Let's pause for just a moment and look inside. What is going on inside you at hearing that Fred was kicked out of the community he had moved across the country to be involved with? Are you experiencing anger? Does part of you say, "What do you expect from religion?!" Has part of you gone into judgment? Just notice. Just observe. When I first heard this story, my reaction was very much one of disgust at what had been done to my friend. It reminded me of my own experience as a youth. Even retelling the tale just now, I felt a small bubble of anger and judgment burst inside of me. The chapter on Forgiveness will be instrumental in dealing with such feelings when they crop up.

⤳

At this point in Fred's story, he was adrift. This is Stage 4 – the spiritual seeker. His church had kicked him out. He had begun to notice aspects of his religion that didn't seem congruent with what he understood his religion to teach. Fred began to look for a new community. The more he looked, the more incongruence he saw. Eventually, Fred felt he had no choice but that of beginning his own church. Rather than giving up his faith, he began making changes where he saw the shortfalls in his previous community and with the most basic teachings of his faith. He started feeding the homeless and caring for people suffering from addiction. No matter who the person was, what they had done, or how they looked or smelled, Fred made sure they had a place where they could go to be loved and to learn about his form of religion.

Rather than finding a new status quo in some other organization, Fred created his own organization to fulfill his need. He has now come full circle, to Stage 5 – arriving at a new status quo. He saw a discrepancy between what the leadership and followers in his previous church were preaching and what they were doing. After being kicked out of that church, he became a pastor himself. He leads his own community and through his leading of that community is learning more and more about his own faith every day.

As traumatic as the experience was for him, Fred recognized it for the blessing it was. While he will tell his story, he will not speak ill of anybody involved in the rumors or his dismissal from the previous church. I have even witnessed him defend the same people who asked him to leave and encourage those complaining about those same people to find love and compassion in their experience. Fred's new status quo is one in which he feels more connected to his faith than ever before.

The experience of this cycle will happen over and over again in our lives, whether we are aware of it or not. It may be happening in many areas of life all at the same time or you may experience it in one area, then another. There are no hard and fast rules in relation to how or where or when this cycle will begin and end.

Chapter Four

## Exploring the Similarities and
## Distinctions of Spirituality and Religion

*I*n their most basic and original intention, religion and spirituality both attempt to help the individual have an experience of divinity. They both want for the individual an awakening to a deeper understanding of the Self. They want the same thing, they just go about it differently.

For many people seeking spirituality, this could be a hard concept to swallow. Many years ago, I would have argued vehemently against such an idea. If you are having a similar reaction, I invite you to keep the beginner's mind active and explore.

While many things could be said about the distinctions between religion and spirituality, this exploration is not intended in any way to indicate that religion is "bad" or that spirituality is "good." Both have their place in the vast arena of human experience. As Shakespeare reminds us, "there is nothing either good or bad, but thinking makes it so."

The purpose of this exploration is not to find differences and create separation. Rather, the purpose is to gain understanding. Many people who seek spirituality do so from a place of frustration with religion. And yet, spirituality is available within religion. It's up to you to discern where your path will lead. It may be down the road of religion or the path of spirituality or both.

## Similarity Between Spirituality and Religion

The primary similarity between spirituality and religion is what they seek for those who participate with them. Both religion and spirituality want people to experience joy, love, freedom, bliss, and peace. Both spirituality and religion seek to improve people's lives and give them a more meaningful context through which to view themselves and their experiences. At the core, their intention and desire is exactly the same.

Coming to this understanding can be very freeing. The intention behind eating an apple or a pear, or anything for that matter, is the same – enjoyable nourishment. If the intention is the same and neither choice is "wrong" or "right" then every option is available to you, and the person who chooses the spinach over the lettuce is simply making a different choice.

## Distinctions Between Spirituality and Religion

If the core intention behind religion and spirituality is the same, the distinctions exist in their views of how to get there. Despite these distinctions, both approaches are valid and valuable. The evidence for this statement is that they exist. If one particular religion was not valid or valuable to anybody, then it would have no followers and cease to be. Like with the example of food, ours is not to judge others for what they find valuable in their growth, but to discover what we find valuable to ours.

In this exploration of the different ways spirituality and religion go about achieving the same intention, these distinctions should be viewed on a spectrum rather than as hard and fast either/or demarcations. Hot and cold are different ends of a temperature spectrum. One particular temperature is no better or worse for where it falls on the spectrum and there is great variety in the "cold" side of the spectrum as well as the "hot."

To generalize, religion has a tendency to fall more on the exclusive side of the spectrum and spirituality tends to land more on the open side. In spirituality, a person can pull ideas and practices from any spiritual philosophy or religion.

Spirituality and religion are not mutually exclusive from the spiritual perspective. A person can be "spiritual but not religious." A Muslim can have their spiritual path within their religion just as the Jew and the Catholic can. A spiritual path can contain teachings from Islam, Christianity, and pagan traditions. There is no limit to what can be a part of a person's spirituality and no limit to the difference in spiritual paths. Each is unique to the individual.

Being a member of a religion, on the other hand, generally requires an individual's exclusive belief and participation in that particular religion. You rarely find, for example, a Jewish Southern Baptist Hindu. This can be very valuable. There is value in landing on one religious system and learning it exclusively for a time. For example, a martial artist who studies karate for three years will be a far more effective martial artist than one who studies karate, kung fu, and taekwondo, each for a one-year span of time.

The use or disuse of dogma is part of this similar intention as well. Merriam-Webster defines dogma as "a belief or set of beliefs that is accepted by the members of a group without being questioned or doubted."

Religion, which tends to ask the student to accept doctrine without question, is based in dogma. By asking a person to accept certain core beliefs without question, religion is seeking to establish that foundation for the individual. It provides a universal framework through which people can have conversations and deepen their understanding of their religion.

Spirituality, on the other hand, generally encourages individuals to find what works for them and use that, while discarding everything else. Spirituality recognizes that demonstration is the only authority, meaning something is only true for the individual if it works for the individual. Religion encourages us to accept its teaching as presented, whereas spirituality encourages us to keep the beginner's mind and check out everything for ourselves.

A group dynamic is essential to religion. This flows from the use of dogma in religious teaching. The entire group tends to believe the same thing, or close to the same thing. This helps to build a sense of community and belonging that can be very important for many people. Spirituality, on the other hand, is very personal. There are as many spiritual paths as there are people on the planet. While there are many similarities between various spiritual paths, each is still unique.

Religion seeks control where spirituality encourages freedom. In religion, there is a certain set of rules and a specified morality. Violation of either of these leads to punishment in one form or another. Again, this is not necessarily "bad." These ideas and practices can be very helpful for some people and may aid them in making choices that are very good choices. Religion also seeks to control belief as well as behavior. Maintaining control over the thought and behavior of people is, from this viewpoint, the best way to help people achieve their aspirations.

Spirituality encourages freedom of thought and behavior as the best way for personal growth. Through their own exploration, the individual discovers what works and what does not work for them. In spirituality, this individual experience is the primary "teacher" of the student.

# Chapter Five

## Redefining Old Church Terms

Nowhere other than in religious terminology is there a more varied understanding of words or more likelihood that a specific word could cause somebody to become upset. For many years if I heard the words "God" or "Jesus," I would feel anger and rage well up inside me. Gladly, this is no longer the case. This experience of anger was caused by the hypocrisy that I perceived in the people who most often used those words. Their definition was much different from mine and their actions even further removed, in my perception, from what they preached. It wasn't until I decided that I got to choose what those words symbolized, and that their meaning to me was independent of what others did with them, that I was able to get past my "allergy."

Defining words in a way that you find supportive is fundamental to creating a spiritual practice that works for you. Once I hit on the idea that I could define words the way I wanted to, new opportunities for learning and growth opened up for me. I was amazed that I had never before realized that I didn't have to accept the definition of the masses, and how freeing it is to set my own definitions. This not only applies to words, but to symbols as well.

The symbol of the cross, for example, is one that I used to find upsetting. This was a big problem because I drove past a giant cross on a hill on my commute to and from my office. Rather than getting upset when I saw this cross, based on what it symbolizes for more traditional religion and my disagreement with that representation, I decided to apply a new meaning. For me, now, the cross symbolizes a roadmap for personal growth.

The vertical line of the cross represents the direction of upward growth. The horizontal line represents the field of polarity – right vs. wrong, good vs. bad, etc. As we grow, we must cross through the field of polarity and remain centered, rather than nailing ourselves to our ideas of "right and wrong." Now, rather than getting upset by this symbol when I see it, I am reminded to do everything I can to stay neutral about my experience.

Your task now is to redefine common terms so that they make more sense and feel more aligned and alive for you. This redefining can also take a word or term from just a concept to something you can actually apply to your life.

The following ideas are the interpretations of these words and ideas that fit best for me. Do not take them blindly, but feel into them. Do they really work for you? If not, what would? Each person's spiritual path is different and each person's definitions of spiritual terms will be different. Have the boldness to pick the meanings that best suit you!

## No Definition Is Perfect

None of the ideas presented here are fully able to capture the depth of meaning behind the terms we'll be exploring. It is not actually possible to fully capture the depth of meaning behind these terms, no matter how they are defined. These are ideas. They grow and expand and become closer and closer to the Truth, but they can only be talked about from our current understanding of them, and given that the depth of these ideas is infinite, there will always be more to understand.

Older ideas of church terminology are not wrong. They exist for a purpose. They work for many, many people. They also don't work for many, many people. If an interpretation doesn't work for me, that doesn't make it bad or wrong, and that interpretation working for somebody else doesn't make it good or right. It just is. However, in order to have a new experience, we need to have a new thought. So don't cling tightly to any idea or interpretation. Let it be loose. As you continually explore the idea, it will shift and grow as you do.

No matter what your previous understanding of these terms may have been, I suggest coming at these ideas with an open mind. As you see the bold heading for each term, do your best to empty your mind of what you previously may have thought related to the term. Be willing to explore these ideas from a place of neutrality.

**God / Spirit / The Universe, etc.:** Your understanding of God is the most fundamental aspect of your spiritual path and practice. The way you perceive God will color everything else. Albert Einstein was very clear on this when he said, "The most important decision we make is whether we believe we live in a friendly or hostile universe." The most important decision we can make is whether God is friendly or hostile. If we decide that God is friendly and allow all of our other thoughts about God to spring from that decision, we will have a very different experience than if we decide God is hostile.

Throughout this book I will use the terms God, Spirit, the Universe, and perhaps others, interchangeably. Centuries have been spent trying to describe and define that which cannot be described or defined. In our best efforts we say that God is infinite, yet even the word infinite conveys a meaning that is capped at our best understanding of what infinite is. We can comprehend up to a certain point and everything beyond that gets the label of "infinite," but the infinite itself is beyond our comprehension.

To assist us in better understanding Spirit or God we can place qualities, or eternal verities, on God. We say things like, God is Unconditional Love. God is Joy, Peace, Bliss, and Grace. God is Compassion and Understanding and Life and Zeal and Wisdom. Inside we can feel into these words and have an experience of them. We can contemplate them and realize that Beauty is Beauty always. The expression of beauty may change but the quality of Beauty is Universal. Our understanding of God will be forever expanding as our consciousness expands along our spiritual journey, but there will always be guideposts to help us be sure we are on the right track. We can use these guideposts to identify if new ideas about God are aligned when they emerge in our awareness. Is the idea inclusive of all or does it separate? Is the idea aligned with Unconditional Love, Life, Joy, Bliss, etc.?

Ascended Masters throughout time and from all religions tell us much the same thing about God. God is birthless, deathless, and changeless. God always has been, always will be and though our understanding of God will grow and change over time, the totality of what God is cannot change because it encompasses everything. Since God encompasses everything, It is completely inclusive, for being everything, God could not exclude any part of Itself. God/Spirit is all there is... ALL there is. There can be no separation, no "other."

Imagine a circle. This circle is infinite. Since this circle is infinite, its center point is everywhere. One inch to your left is the center of this circle. Two feet above your head is the center of this circle. One billion light-years away is the center of this circle. The circumference or surrounding edge of this circle is nowhere. If everywhere you look you find the center of the circle, then its edge can never be found and must then not exist. This circle represents God.

Now, in your imagination, try to get outside of the circle. You can't do it. Wherever in the circle you go, you are in the center of the circle. God is not separate from us, nor are we separate from God. Everybody exists in God and is an inseparable piece of God, despite how easy it is to feel separate.

In your mind's eye, imagine the ocean. There are waves upon the surface of this ocean. Where does the wave stop and the ocean start? Is not the wave inseparable from the ocean? If you could scoop up the wave in a bucket, it would cease to be a wave and just be water in a bucket. The ocean would be diminished; it would be missing that wave.

Symbolically this is true of our relationship with Spirit. If Spirit is the ocean, then we are the wave. We exist as part of the ocean and cannot be taken from the ocean. As the wave, all that we are is ocean, yet the ocean is far more vast than the wave. And so it is with you. All that you are is God, but God is far more than what you are. This is a mighty concept to grasp but I urge you to sit with it for a while and explore it.

While there are several differences between a religious and spiritual interpretation of God, let's explore this idea from a point of agreement between religion and spirituality. Both religion and spirituality tend to have four significant understandings about God in common: God is omnipresence and omnipresent (existing everywhere),

God is omniscience and omniscient (all knowledge and all knowing), God is omnipotence and omnipotent (all power and all powerful), and God is Unconditional Love.

## Omnipresent

Beginning with the idea of God being omnipresent, it becomes clear that all we are is God. Omnipresent means to be everywhere present. Thus, God is present in the room where you currently find yourself. God must also be present inside every cell of your body, inside every nucleus of every cell of your body, inside every atom of that nucleus, inside every sub-atomic particle and inside the very "field of potential" from which quantum science tells us everything originates. If God is indeed omnipresent then all that I am and all that you are is God.

## Omniscient

The idea of omniscience says that God "knows" everything and *is* everything there is to be known. God is knowledge itself. The unlimited nature of God extends to knowledge. There is no limit to what is "known" in, as, and through God. You are a part of this infinite knowing, just as you are a part of God Itself. Being connected to all knowing, you are able to know anything and everything there is to know. You are connected to it and are a part of it. Nothing is unknowable to you.

Have you ever had a brilliant idea for a new product only to see it on the store shelves a few months later? What is knowable anywhere is knowable everywhere. This is what the omniscience, which all religions agree to about God, means.

## Omnipotent

Being omnipotent and omnipotence means that God is all power and all powerful. This completely eliminates the existence, or even the possibility of the existence, of Satan or the devil as force for evil. If God is all power, how can there be an opposite power opposing God? There can't.

Abraham Lincoln spoke wise words in his House Divided Speech when he said, "A house divided against itself cannot stand." A Oneness (God) divided against itself ceases to exist. So where does this leave us? Are we nothing more than pawns at the whim of all powerful God? Not at all. God is all powerful because God is the source of all power. Within our own lives, we have the authority to work within the laws of creation (discussed in greater depth later) to create our experience.

## Unconditional Love

All religions agree that God is Unconditional Love. A later chapter is dedicated to the discussion of what this means.

Our oneness with Spirit is what allows us the potential for growth. If we were not made of the same "stuff" as God, then we would be finite and our growth potential would be severely capped. However, God is infinite. I am one with and a part of God and as such, I too am infinite. Think back to before you were able to walk. Did the you of today seem at all possible to the you who was learning to walk? The you of today was not even an imagination of that baby and yet here you are.

Just as the baby-you could not even begin to comprehend or imagine the you of today, so the you of today cannot even begin to comprehend or imagine the true potential of you in the future.

## The Old Man in the Sky

God and Spirit are used interchangeably, though it might be easier with the usage of "Spirit" to eliminate the image of God as an old man in the sky. God is human in that we are human and we are a part of God. By the same token, God is bird, horse, stone, and wind. In our explorations of the meaning of "God," doing everything possible to release the ideas of God as the old man in the sky is vital. Beginning with the idea of God as a concept rather than a "thing" can be very helpful.

## The Universe / One Song

The term "Universe" is also often used in place of God or Spirit. Universe represents wholeness. Uni – meaning "one" is combined with "verse" or song – one song. Everything in creation is part of the same song, the same harmony, the same wholeness. Albert Einstein put it this way: "A human being is a part of the whole, called by us the 'Universe'..." As a part of the whole we can't be separated from the whole, no matter how separate we may seem. Einstein continues, "He experiences himself, his thoughts and feelings as something separated from the rest, a kind of optical delusion of his consciousness." Your spiritual practice, and the recognition that the music note cannot be separate from the song it harmonizes, will help to heal this misperception.

**I Am / Self / Life, etc.:** Throughout this book you will notice certain words beginning with a capital letter that are usually started in the lowercase. This is an indication that a higher idea is being conveyed. If I use Self, I am referring to the aspect of the individual that is the true nature of who and what we are, not the jumbled-up mix of thoughts, feelings, concerns, fear, etc. from which people generally operate.

"I Am" is a name for Spirit. "I am" generally relates to more basic, physical level understanding. For example, "I am hungry" gives a description of a need of the physical body. "I Am perfectly at peace" means that the divine spark that is me, which could be called soul, is perfectly at peace regardless of how the physical world experiences may seem. It is a spiritual truth, rather than a physical experience.

The use of capital and lowercase letters is not meant to convey separation. It could be easy to assume that there is the lower self and the higher Self and that they are two separate things, but this is not so. "I Am" is always the truth of my divine nature. "I am" is the mask I put over that divine nature.

**Heaven and Hell:** While many religions teach that Heaven and Hell are physical locations in which we will one day take up permanent residence, the spiritual perspective is that they are metaphors rather than actual places. The idea of Heaven and Hell as physical places is very effective if the intention is to control behavior. There is no better carrot than Heaven and there is no more fearful stick than Hell. The carrot and stick method can be very effective for many people in helping them to live their life by a certain standard, but they are not aligned with the freedom of exploration encouraged by spirituality.

Retired Episcopal Bishop John Shelby Spong in an interview said, "... if you have Heaven as a place where you're rewarded for your goodness and Hell as a place where you're punished for your evil, then you sort of have control of the population. And so they create this fiery place which has quite literally scared the Hell out of a lot of people throughout Christian history, and it's part of a control tactic." By looking at the ideas of Heaven and Hell from a spiritual perspective, we can liberate ourselves from this control tactic and participate more freely in our own spiritual advancement.

From the spiritual perspective, Heaven and Hell do exist, but not as separate places where we go for reward or punishment. Heaven and Hell exist here and now as our inner experience of life, based upon how we interpret the things that happen around us. Everybody has had a "hellish experience" or described something as "heavenly." When somebody says, "It was hell," they are describing an experience of the state of mind that is hell. When somebody says, "That was just heavenly," they are describing the experience of the state of mind that is heaven.

One well-known mystic once said that the Kingdom of Heaven is within. We access that kingdom through our spiritual practice, by learning how to free ourselves from limiting interpretations of what happens around us. Rather than waiting until after leaving this incarnation to experience heaven, you can cultivate a consciousness that brings heavenly experiences to your everyday life.

**Jesus:** While there are no verifiable birth certificates, it is fairly safe to assume that Yeshua bar Yosef (Jesus, son of Joseph) was a historical figure that walked the planet roughly 2,000 plus years ago. Both spirituality and religion agree that such a person existed and taught religion/ spirituality. The primary difference between religion and spirituality in relation to Jesus is one word. Religion calls Jesus the Great Exception while spirituality refers to him as the Great Example.

In the typical religious (Christian) viewpoint, Jesus is set aside as special. He is not only the Son of God but is actually God incarnate. The rest of us are merely human. This creates the illusion of separation. In redefining God, the context was set that there is no separation. We can't be separate from the "allness" that God is and so Jesus could not inherently be any better than anybody else. He was just more aware of his oneness with Spirit.

In fact, nothing Jesus is reported to have said indicates that he is any different from the rest of us. Quite the contrary, the quote "...the works that I do, [you] will do also; and greater works than these [you] will do," implies that Jesus himself believed that we are on equal footing with him, or else how could we do greater works?

The quote, "I am the way, and the truth, and the life..." is often used to justify Jesus as separate and better than the rest of us. Yet when the burning bush told Moses, "I Am that I Am," God was proclaiming a name for Itself. That name is, I Am. So the quote from Jesus has nothing to do with the personal self, but rather should read, "God is the way, and the truth, and the life..." Remember, God is all there is, so God, as the I Am in Jesus, that is "the way and the truth and the life," is the I Am in you and me.

It is far more empowering to think of Jesus in the spiritual context, as the Great Example of what is possible for humanity (not the Great Exception). In spirituality, Jesus is often referred to as the Master Teacher. He followed his spiritual path so far as to become more aligned with his own divinity than anybody else. Certainly very few others history is aware of, such as Buddha and Krishna, have reached such levels of spiritual attunement.

His accomplishment was extraordinary, but something of which all of us are capable. In fact, his life was dedicated to showing the people of his day, and every age to follow, how to align with the divinity inside, like he did.

**Christ:** Contrary to popular belief, Christ was not Jesus' last name. It is a title. Just like Buddha was not The Buddha's first name, but a title, so too Christ was a title given to Jesus in recognition of his spiritual attainment.

In spirituality, the Christ is referred to as the true nature of each of us. The Christ is that spark of divinity that we truly are. It is the Christ within that Ram Dass spoke of when he said, "When you know how to listen, everyone is the guru." Everyone can be the guru because everyone has within them the same Christ presence.

It is the Christ within that we are seeking to express more of through our spiritual practice. It is given equally to all people, regardless of race, religion, gender, sexuality or belief. It is our High-Self or our Spirit. When the Bible refers to "Christ in you, the hope of glory," it has nothing to do with the personage of Jesus but rather the inexhaustible Light at the core of your being.

Just as "I Am" is a name for God, so too is Christ a name for God as an individual expression of Spirit, fully awake in the world. Jesus knew himself as Christ, which is to say, as one with God. Not all of God, but a full and complete individualized expression of God. The Truth of you and me and everybody on the planet is that Christ-Self.

Very few people are ready to open to that idea. Even fewer are bold enough to explore it. However, within you right now is that Christ presence. It has always been there, it will always be there. That same Christ presence is in everyone and at some point, we all will awaken to the Christ within.

**Sin:** Sin is a big, bad thing in traditional religion. Everybody sins, is a sinner, and must atone and seek forgiveness. In redefining sin, it is best to look at the original meaning of the word. The word that was translated into sin from the original Greek is hamartia, which means to "miss the mark." It was an archery term indicating that you failed to hit your target. Ernest Holmes, the founder of Religious Science says "There is no sin but a mistake and no punishment but an inevitable consequence." It is simple cause and effect, choice and consequence, action and result. If a person drinks too much, they will have a hangover.

Sin, as viewed from the original definition of "missing the mark" is far less devastating than the religious interpretation. If an archer misses the target, the wise archer reviews the last shot to discover what adjustment needs to be made, draws the bow again, and shoots true. In this context, "sin" provides an opportunity for learning.

Instead of the sport of archery, consider basketball. If a basketball player misses a free throw and says, "I am awful and terrible person, being so disgraceful as to miss a free throw," is that player very likely to make the next one? No. The shooter is more likely to miss again, and again, and again. If instead this person thinks, "Hmm.... it seems like I could use a little bit more height on my shot next time," they will pick up the ball, shoot again, and improve.

If we view sin as more than just a mistake, it has the tendency to cascade and become a self-fulfilling prophecy. If I miss a free throw and say to myself, "There is no sin but a mistake (my shot was off) and no punishment but an inevitable consequence (I missed the basket)," it ends right there. If I judge myself as a terrible basketball player because I missed the shot, I have just stacked another mistake (or sin) on top by judging myself. This will likely lead to more missed shots, which will lead to more self-judgment, and on and on.

It is very, very important to get clear on this idea because it can free you from incredible amounts of unnecessary torment. God does not tally up our sins and think up punishments to fit our crimes. We do this to ourselves as we judge ourselves.

Included in our "sins" are the "punishments" or consequences, just as included in our good deeds are our rewards. If we learn from our mistakes, we do not repeat them. If we don't, we will repeat them until we do. When we no longer make the same mistake, we will cease to be "punished" for it.

**Punishment:** Punishment is an idea often talked about in traditional religion. I recommend removing the idea of divine punishment from your spiritual vocabulary.

God is not concerned with punishment. Punishment is a purely human invention. Spirit's only concern is in balance and harmony. This is achieved through the simple and well-known law of cause and effect.

We all learned about cause and effect in school and while it is a law of the natural world, it is also a law in the spiritual world. Everything we do is a cause that sets in motion an effect. The effect is not a punishment or a reward, but the natural outcome of the cause that was set in motion. If we put a pot of water on a stove to boil it, the water boiling is the natural result. If we forget to turn on the burner, the water not boiling isn't our punishment. It's just what happens when water is not heated. The same is true for God/Spirit/the Universe. There is no such thing as punishment, just the outcome of cause and effect.

The Universe is harmonious and in order for that harmony to be maintained, everything must be balanced, and will be.

**Karma:** Karma, an idea prominent in Eastern philosophies, is simply another term for cause and effect. The idea of Karma can be taken to an extreme and become a sneaky way of saying "punishment." I have often heard people say "instant karma" when something negative happens right on the heels of an action they deem to be negative.

For example, Steve accidentally bumps into Jane. Jane becomes upset and yells at Steve to pay attention to where he is going. Jane turns to leave and bumps into Dan, who is carrying a cup of coffee that gets spilled on Jane. Steve then says, "Instant karma!" This situation illustrates how the idea of karma can be perceived as a substitute for punishment. Steve is overjoyed that Jane bumped into Dan and got covered in coffee. "It serves her right!"

Karma, as the term will be used in this book, simply means cause and effect. In the example of Steve, Jane, and Dan, it may well be karma (cause and effect) at play that had a hand in the way Jane ran into Dan. It may not have. We can't know one way or the other. However, if karma (cause and effect) was doing its thing, it was not about punishment, it was about balance.

Furthermore, Steve's satisfaction with Jane getting doused with hot coffee will set karma in motion in his experience as well and could bring about results that he probably will not be fond of. This would not be as a punishment, but as a balancing of the vindictive energy he put out. What we put out comes back to us…always.

Karma (cause and effect) is often invoked in the negative. If something bad happens, it's karma. When somebody does something bad, karma is going to get them. The truth is that cause and effect does not deal in good or bad, just cause and effect.

If the cause that is set in motion is generosity, then generosity will be the effect. If aggression is set in motion, aggression will be returned. Good and bad are human ideas and have nothing to do with spirituality. In spirituality, things simply are. Again, from William Shakespeare, "for there is nothing either good or bad, but thinking makes it so."

This does not necessarily mean that we are doomed to meet a terrible fate from our past actions. Everything we do engages Karma to one degree or another. Through forgiveness work (discussed in a later chapter) and other spiritual practices, the cause and effect cycle can be mitigated.

**Acceptance:** Acceptance can be a confusing term. We often hear, "just accept it," as an instruction to shut up and take it, whatever "it" may be. Acceptance, as it is typically understood, often carries with it the energy of resignation. Whatever it is that you are accepting is something you can't do anything about, so you'd better get used to it. This is not at all acceptance in the spiritual context.

In the spiritual context, acceptance simply means recognizing that what is, is. Acceptance is neutral. It doesn't make any situation right or wrong. It doesn't mean giving up and resigning yourself to a fate beyond your control. It simply says, "Okay, this is in my experience. I accept that this is in my experience. Now, what do I want to do with it?"

John-Roger, founder of the Church of the Movement of Spiritual Inner Awareness (MSIA) says that "acceptance is the first law of Spirit." Spiritually speaking, our first task, in any situation, is to come into acceptance. The alternative to acceptance is resistance.

As a very simple example, imagine you go to a bakery to buy a chocolate chip cookie. When you walk in the door you notice that they are sold out of chocolate chip cookies. You could go into resistance, get upset, and yell at the clerk for running out of chocolate chip cookies. After all of this resistance, the bakery will still be sold out of chocolate chip cookies. Or, you can choose acceptance.

Acceptance recognizes that there are no chocolate chip cookies to be had at this particular bakery and allows you the space to choose to either 1) pick a different cookie, 2) go to a different bakery, or 3) not have a cookie after all. Acceptance brings you choices. Resistance crowds out your awareness of the choices you have. Acceptance keeps you in the present, which is the only place where you have any power. Resistance locks you either in the past or in some imagined and undesirable future, where you have zero power.

**Coincidence vs. Synchronicity:** The events in our lives can be viewed either as coincidence or synchronicity. Coincidence implies two events that seem connected are really random and unrelated. From the spiritual perspective, there is no such thing as a disconnected anything. Everything and everyone is connected in some regard or another. Nothing is random. Everything has a cause and everything that comes into our experience is connected to us in some way.

Synchronicity, on the other hand, implies that everything is connected and very purposefully so. For example, consider a cell phone ringing during a lecture right at the key point the lecturer is intending to convey. Is this random and meaningless, or is it purposeful, serving to provide extra emphasis for those choosing to recognize it as synchronistic, rather than annoying and disruptive? Synchronicity acknowledges the interconnected nature of the Universe. From the perspective of synchronicity, we can feel supported by Spirit and build our faith. Choosing to view something as coincidence may perhaps give you a good story, but will do little for you spiritually.

**Faith:** Often times when people say "faith" what they really mean is a good deal of doubt and fear glossed over with a dash of hope. This type of "faith" is far better than nothing, but is also far from what I consider the real meaning of faith to be.

The Bible has a wonderful quote on faith. From the George Lamsa translation, Hebrews 11:1 states "Now faith is the substance of things hoped for, just as it was the substance of things which have come to pass; and it is the evidence of things not seen." That seems like a very heady quote, but once it's broken down a bit it really brings faith into perspective.

There are many definitions of substance. Check out this one from Merriam-Webster: "Ultimate reality that underlies all outward manifestations and change." So, faith is the ultimate reality behind the stuff we hope for and everything we have ever had. We could boil it down even more. Faith is reality. That which you have faith in is what is in your experience.

Everybody has faith. Everybody has perfect faith. The question becomes, where is that faith placed? The answer is as simple to discover as looking at life. What manifests in your life shows you where you place your perfect faith. If you struggle to find a relationship, then your faith is placed in struggle around finding a relationship. If you find that your finances are always more than enough then your faith is placed in your supply meeting your needs.

You are always using 100% of your faith. As a function of your consciousness, your faith is always active, all the time. Your choice lies in how you use that faith. If you remain on autopilot, you will continue to receive what you've always received. Through a spiritual practice, you can more powerfully and consciously choose how you use your faith through the increased awareness and more expansive consciousness that results from your practice.

Returning to the Bible quote, the second half indicates that faith is "the evidence of things not seen." Everything that is currently seen was once unseen. Before anything was a thing, it was first an idea. In order for the idea to become a thing, somebody had to catch it and act on it. Many people will grab hold of an idea at that same time, but most will never do anything with the idea. This is because they haven't put their faith in the idea and their ability to execute it. Faith, being the "evidence of things not seen," is what inspires and drives the inventor forward in their creation of the idea. To the one who brings an idea to creation, the "thing" was real even though it was still "not seen."

Faith is not hoping. Faith is certainty. Most people don't choose where to put that faith. When not consciously used, our faith seems to default to doubt, fear, and unbelief. It is a habit ingrained in us by the society we were born into, which is largely unconscious of its own habit. The spiritual practices discussed in Part II of this book will provide the foundation upon which you can begin to consciously direct your faith.

**Immortality and Reincarnation:** Traditional Christian doctrine teaches that our immortality comes into play after we die on Earth. Our physical life is limited yet once we die we are born to eternal life, either in the bliss of Heaven or the torment of Hell.

In Spirituality, immortality is quite different. The Tibetan Book of the Dead is quoted as saying, "We came from the light, we put on a coat of skins and we shall return to the light." This quote implies a cyclical nature. If we first came from the Light, but chose to put on a coat of skins, when we return to the Light it seems quite likely that we will have the choice to put on yet another coat of skins.

Remember, in spirituality, God/Spirit is all there is and as such, there is no place to "go" when our physical bodies cease to function. We are already immersed in God. The Soul, without a body, is still immersed in God.

From the perspective of spirituality, the whole point of incarnating, or putting on the coat of skins, is to gain experience. Try as you might, you cannot adequately describe how a peach tastes. The only way to understand what it is like to eat a peach is to eat a peach. The only way for us, as immortal and spiritual beings to learn about ourselves is through experience. Thus, we take on a body for a time to learn and experience all we can. When the body no longer functions, it is released and we return to the Light before taking on another body.

Exploring the idea of immortality can become tricky because we must eventually bring in the word infinite, which we already know is unknowable to the limited human brain. The infinite nature of Spirit includes the possibility of infinite experiences. I must actually eat a peach to know what eating a peach is like. By my experience of eating the peach, I come to know myself better and have taken a step on the road to "Know Thyself." Given that the only way to truly know yourself is to experience all of yourself, and that by the nature of the infinite there are limitless experiences of yourself to have, you must be immortal and continually find body after body after body.

In a Universe of infinite possibility that body may be a human body, but it may be a very different body. When you dream, do you not sometimes inhabit a body that is very different from your waking body? Again, we run into the idea of the infinite. With infinite possibility for infinite experience, there are infinite possibilities for "coats of skin."

**Race Consciousness:** The term "race consciousness" refers to the conglomeration of human consciousness on the planet. In one sense it is an average. Consciousness, as related to the individual, will be discussed in more depth in Chapter 6. The combined total of all individual consciousness makes up the race consciousness. Everybody is a part of the race consciousness and, to the degree that you allow it, the combined consciousness of the entire planet will govern your life and experience.

Until somebody decides to take responsibility for their own consciousness, the weight of the masses will have greater pull than anything else. If the majority of the planet is living in fear, the unconscious person will be subject to that fear and most, if not all of their experience, will be filtered through generalized fear. Race consciousness does not trend towards the positive.

⁓

There will be more terms redefined along the way. The main thing to keep in mind is that you should always substitute a term that works for you. If you don't like the word "God" for example and prefer "Spirit" then mentally replace any instance of God in this book with the word Spirit. Your spiritual practice is far too important to allow it to be hijacked by words you don't like. It may be difficult at first, but with practice, mentally replacing one word for another will become habit, and eventually, the "allergy," or internal negative reaction, to the original word will disappear.

# Chapter Six

## Consciousness

Spiritual teachings tend to throw around the word "consciousness" a lot but don't often discuss what consciousness really means. Truly understanding what consciousness is, how it is created, and how it's changed is of vital importance. The whole purpose of a spiritual practice is to improve and expand your consciousness. This chapter is devoted to exploring what consciousness is, what consciousness does, and how consciousness is created or improved.

## What Is Consciousness?

Consciousness seems at the surface level to be fairly simple, but it is really quite complex. Your individual consciousness is the sum total of everything you have ever said, thought, felt or done. That's not too hard of a concept to grasp, right? Well, that sum total of everything you have ever said, thought, felt or done includes this and every other incarnation. It includes things from this incarnation that you are aware of and things that are operating in the background of your subconscious mind.

As mentioned earlier, spirituality says that God is all there is. ALL there is. There is nothing that is not included in the Allness of Spirit and so there is no "where" for a thought, feeling, word, or action to "go." They originate from you and stay with you. It all goes in your "bucket" labeled consciousness and that "bucket" determines your every experience.

If, for example, you grew up having a negative experience of eating peas, then as an adult you will likely avoid trying a dish containing peas, no matter how good everybody says it is. If you grew up loving peas, you are more likely to try said dish. This is a very simplistic example of how consciousness works to create our every experience. Even just with the idea of peas, your thoughts about the people you ate peas with as a child figure into the mix. If your uncle was a pea farmer and you spent a summer with him working the farm, those experiences will also figure into your sum total of consciousness around something as simple as peas, from just this incarnation.

The good news is that all of the items in your consciousness bucket are not weighted the same. Everything carries its own energy or vibration and some vibrations are higher than others. This allows many negative entries into the consciousness bucket to be balanced out by fewer positive entries. One experience of forgiveness can counteract many experiences of judgment.

This is very good news because it means that you don't necessarily need to go exploring down to the bottom of your bucket to see what's there. You just need to do your very best to put high-vibrational experiences into the bucket.

While it is possible to counter-balance our negative consciousness entries without digging them up, it's likely during the process of growth that specific things will rise to surface. This is also very good news. If specific things come up for your attention, you can put your efforts toward directly clearing those particular things.

To explore this a bit further, let's assume that Jane wants to have more money. Jane knows that her consciousness around money, wealth, abundance, prosperity, etc. is creating her experience of these areas of life and that if she wants a different experience she will need to up-level her consciousness. The only way for Jane to do this is with focused attention and effort.

Jane begins by deciding that she needs to notice abundance around her more often. Abundance can show up in many ways. Abundance doesn't always mean money. There is an abundance of grass in a field, an abundance of sand on the beach, and an abundance of leaves on a tree.

So, Jane begins to look for abundance surrounding her in her daily life. She goes to the beach and thinks to herself, "I am standing on an abundance of sand. Sand is all around me. There are more grains of sand under my feet than I could ever count and the sand goes on for as far as I can see. I am literally standing on and surrounded by abundance!" This is a very powerful experience of abundance that goes into her consciousness bucket and counteracts many previous thoughts of lack. Every time Jane does this, she is conditioning her consciousness to accept abundance as normal and natural.

After a while of this practice, seemingly out of the blue, Jane remembers an experience she had when she was eight years old. While heading out for dinner with her parents, the family car was rear-ended by a very expensive luxury car. The driver of that car was irate, yelling and blaming Jane's parents, when they had done nothing wrong.

From this, Jane's first direct experience of somebody with wealth, eight-year-old Jane decided that rich people are mean and nasty. From a child's perspective this makes sense and, from Jane's very limited experience of rich people, was 100% true to her. The belief that rich people are jerks was filed away in Jane's subconscious and became an unconscious influence, coloring her every experience of wealth and wealthy people.

Having decided that rich people are mean, subconsciously and automatically, Jane began to look for proof that rich people are indeed mean. Seek and ye shall find. Unconsciously, this belief helped to limit Jane's experience of abundance. After all, if rich people are jerks and I want to be nice, that means I can't be rich, right?

So, here we come back to adult Jane, who has been working on changing her consciousness around money. Jane has been at work noticing abundance all around her and recognizing that abundance is normal and natural. All of that work paved the way for her subconscious belief that rich people are bad people to surface and be addressed. While Jane continues to work with more generic consciousness-elevating practices around abundance and money, she can now specifically address this false belief that has been coloring her experience since she was eight years old.

When you seek to change your consciousness, the generic work supports you in preparing the way for the specific work. A hiking trail to the mountain must be cut before the mountain can be climbed. Once the mountain has been climbed, the hiker has a new vista from which to see his or her way forward and then begin clearing another trail to the next mountain. I recognize that this metaphor makes this work sound daunting. But rest assured, while it can be intense, the results are well worth it.

Looking back along the way they have come, the hiker can see every other mountain they have climbed. Jane will always know that as an eight-year-old she decided rich people were mean. She will always know that this belief kept her from her own experience of wealth until she changed it, and from the bow of her 50-foot yacht, gazing into the sunset over the Aegean Sea, she will look back on her journey and be filled with joy and gratitude for every single step.

So how is all of this related to crafting a spiritual practice? It is our consciousness that creates our experience. If the goal of a spiritual practice is complete emancipation from all discord of every nature, and your consciousness creates your experience, then any discord you experience is a direct result of your consciousness. The spiritual practice you craft and participate in will be one that elevates your consciousness.

Knowing how consciousness works is vital in your spiritual work because changing consciousness *is* your spiritual work. When you run into roadblocks along the way, realizing that what is before you was always within you, and now is ready to be released, gives a completely different perspective on struggles.

# Part II

# Spiritual Practices

Thank you for taking the time to explore Part I. Keep in mind, the discussion of the topics covered in Part I, while setting the context for Part II, just scratches the surface. Entire books could be written about each of the chapters covered so far. For that matter, entire books could be written about each chapter yet to come. I encourage you to continue to contemplate what has been presented so far as time goes on. The more you think about something, the more likely you are to have a new thought about it, and it is only new thoughts that move you forward.

Speaking of the chapters yet to come, from here on this book is dedicated to the exploration of nine different spiritual practices. This may seem like a lot at first, but not to worry – they are all very inter-related as you will come to see. These nine practices do not represent all of the possible tools that are available to you, but from my perspective they are all critical to a robust spiritual practice.

# Chapter Seven

# Components of a Spiritual Practice

*E*very individual has great flexibility in crafting their own spiritual practice, and yet there are several core practices that are vital to having a robust spiritual practice. Nine of these will be explored in the remaining chapters. They include: Prayer, Affirmations, Love, Compassion, Visualization and Manifestation, Meditation, Forgiveness, Gratitude, and Spiritual Education. Nine spiritual practices may seem like a lot, however participating in all of them, daily, is very easy to accomplish. And yes, eventually, ideally, you will participate in your spiritual practice every single day...including weekends, vacations, and holidays.

"Eventually" is the key word. Beginning right where you are is the most important thing. If all you can imagine in this moment is spending five minutes once a week working on a spiritual practice, then begin with five minutes once a week.

Make it okay to be right where you are. You couldn't start from anywhere else anyway. I started right where I was.

I had known about spirituality and spiritual practices for my entire life, yet had no practice. I thought so poorly of myself that in my mind, only if I were wealthy would anybody even pretend to love me, and I was willing to settle for that. I stood in one of the darkest corners of the basement of a spiritual center, silently begging somebody, anybody, to say hello to me before I walked out, being just as lost as before. Somebody did say hello and I decided to come back, one more time.

That was my starting point, one more visit. And then another. And then another. One Sunday, the minister suggested coming to a class, so I signed up for a short class, and then another. Those basic classes led to countless spiritual counseling sessions, and more in-depth classes. Those classes led to my own licensure as a spiritual counselor, to a seat on the Board of Trustees for that spiritual center, and then to my election as President of the Board. My spiritual practice led me to a Master's degree in Spiritual Psychology, a career speaking and teaching spirituality, and to writing and publishing books. It will lead me to even more amazing experiences in the future.

Where will your spiritual practice lead you? The only way to know is to begin it and see.

## What Counts as a Spiritual Practice

The interesting thing about crafting your own spiritual practice is that there is no limit to what can be considered part of it. There are really only two requirements: 1) Does the tool/practice help you to feel more connected to Spirit; and 2) Does it harm no one, no thing, and seek only the Highest good of all? If the answers are yes, then it counts. If you find that gardening brings you a feeling of being one with Life and you feel uplifted and inspired while gardening to think about God, then by all means include gardening as part of your spiritual practice. Paramahansa Yogananda, the founder of Self-Realization Fellowship, said, "We should read a little, meditate more, and think of God all the time." If you have an easier and more natural time thinking about God or feeling connected to Spirit while doing a particular task, that task for you is spiritual.

Another thing to consider about qualifying some particular tool or task as spiritual, is really the intention and attention we bring to it. Imagine two people picking up trash on the side of the road. While one of them is just picking up trash, the intention of the other person is to be a consciously beneficial presence to the planet and serve Spirit through picking up the trash. The only difference between the two is the mindset that is brought to the task at hand. The one with the mindset of serving Spirit is engaged in their spiritual practice, while the other is not. Said another way, it is the consciousness of the individual that makes the act spiritual or not.

## Qualities of Spiritual Tools

Qualities are also very important when it comes to defining spiritual tools; more specifically, qualities of God and therefore your true Self. As mentioned in Part I, the qualities of God (sometimes called eternal verities) are qualities that have always existed, will always exist, and while their expression may vary, the quality itself is always the same. Beauty is a great example. The sunset is beautiful. A fully bloomed passion flower is beautiful. These are different representations of beauty, but the idea of beauty remains the same.

While universal in one sense, eternal verities are also quite personal. One individual may find a particular painting to be beautiful while another may not care for the same work, so beauty in that sense is personal. And yet, while I may not find a particular painting beautiful,

I completely understand what somebody else means when they call it beautiful.

Activities that cultivate experiences of eternal verities can be considered spiritual practices. Once again, however, consciousness is the key. If I go to a museum to look at art and experience great beauty but it stops there, while I may have had a wonderful and uplifting time, it would not necessarily constitute a spiritual practice. However, if I take that experience of beauty and ride it into musings on Spirit, then I am engaged in spiritual practice. For me, it might sound something like...

> *Wow! This painting is so beautiful. How did the artist ever think up that combination of colors? It must have been inspired. Hundreds of years ago, this artist opened up enough to Spirit to allow inspiration to flow through them, through the brush and the paints and onto the canvas. And here I stand, hundreds of years later, witnessing with my eyes God working through man. I didn't partake in that spiritual experience hundreds of years ago and yet I am partaking in it right now. How blessed I am to be able to see this. This is truly a gift. Thank you, God. Thank you, Spirit!*

Clearly, there is quite a difference between that experience and "Oh, the paintings were very beautiful." Experiencing beauty, or any other eternal verity for that matter, is a wonderful thing of itself, to be sure. But that doesn't necessarily qualify it as a spiritual practice.

## Nix the Quick Fix

Spirituality is not a quick fix system. While there may be very quick fixes in your experience, you will get the most out of your spiritual practice if you undertake it as a life-long adventure. After having been raised on spirituality and more than a decade of consistent, dedicated practice, I have experienced phenomenal results and know quite clearly that despite all my experiences and successes, I have barely scratched the surface of what is possible. I have come far enough to realize how far there is yet to go, but I have also come far enough to know that every single step will be delicious!

# Chapter Eight

# Spiritual Practice: Affirmative Prayer

Prayer is a vital component of any spiritual practice. It allows us a way to communicate with Spirit and build a sense of rapport with the Universe. We are already in perfect rapport with the Universe, our awareness is all that is missing. Prayer helps to fill your consciousness bucket in the way you desire. Prayer can help shift your experience from desperation to joy and bring extra confidence into play.

Prayer is practiced very differently in spirituality than in religion (and even among different spiritual life philosophies), and that difference stems from the understanding of what is being prayed to. The spiritually redefined idea of "God" is significantly different from the traditional interpretation of most religions, and our ideas of prayer need to be updated to match.

For the time being, forget everything you have learned about prayer in the past and bring the beginner's mind into play. In order to establish an empowering and effective style of prayer, it must be clear what is being prayed to and how what is being prayed to operates. Previously we began to explore the idea of being that which God is. So, how do we pray to what we are? As odd and potentially sacrilegious as this might sound, how would you pray to you? From the beginner's mind, explore and play with that question. How would I pray to me?

Would I pray to me in supplication?

> *Dear Ben, I am such a bad Ben and, Ben, I know I don't deserve a second chance, but Me, if You would just give me a second chance, I promise I will change and do good!*

That doesn't really work, does it?

Praying to myself like that makes me feel terrible. A prayer in supplication assumes that the prayer is going to a God that needs to be cajoled, a God that might say "yes" or "no" depending on a whim. Remember, religion and spirituality agree that God is Unconditional Love. Unconditional Love does not need to be convinced that a person praying has suffered enough or is sincere enough about changing.

Instead, I would pray to myself in affirmation.

> *Dear Ben, I know that You are in me and I am in You and that we are inseparably one. And so, I give thanks for my answered prayer.*

That feels much better to me. Prayer in a spiritual context is affirmative prayer, meaning that the answer to the prayer is affirmed in the prayer itself.

Imagine that you desire an apple. Included in the desire for the apple is the answer to the desire for the apple. In my recognition of my desire for an apple, I get up and go get an apple. In praying to myself for an apple, I don't need to convince myself that I have suffered from my hunger long enough to deserve to have an apple. I simply eat an apple.

Now, let's allow that simplistic example to expand into the greater idea of Spirit that was presented earlier. God is all there is. I must therefore be a part of God. My desire must also be a part of God, because God is all there is. If my desire is financial abundance, then I am already one with that financial abundance because I am a part of God and financial abundance is also a part of God.

I do not need to convince God that I deserve financial abundance because from the perspective of God I am already connected to financial abundance. Rather, I need to convince MYSELF that I deserve financial abundance. The withholding is not from God. God cannot withhold a part of itself any more than you can withhold the oxygen from your last breath from any part of your body that requires it. From this perspective, praying to myself really isn't sacrilege or inaccurate at all.

The purpose of prayer is to so convince yourself of your desires as a present reality that you automatically open to receive those desires. The source from which we all receive is Spirit. Spirit is the only source of anything because It is everything. We are an integral part of Spirit, meaning that we are already connected to that for which we pray. All we need to do is to open to receive it and take the necessary action in the physical world to bring it to us.

In order for prayer to be affirmative, it must assume and accept that the prayer is already answered. This does not mean that I pray for financial abundance and then open my eyes expecting a pile of money to have magically appeared in front of me. Rather, my prayer for financial abundance would affirm that I already am connected to financial abundance, and that I accept that abundance to a greater degree than ever before. This prayer would go into my consciousness bucket. The more fully I convinced myself with my prayer and the more enthusiastically I prayed, the greater impact it will have on the sum total of my consciousness as related to abundance.

As my consciousness shifts so too does my experience. Rather than expecting a pile of money to have magically appeared before me during my prayer, I would begin looking into my experience and the world around me with the intention of seeing and experiencing greater abundance in any way abundance can show up, and in particular, financially.

The spiritual practice of affirmative prayer, by adding to your consciousness bucket, helps to expand your consciousness. As your consciousness expands, so does your experience. It is affirmative prayer that forms the mold for what you seek to create in your experience. Through detailed and consistent prayer work, you direct your subconscious mind and inform the Universe of your intentions. Working with affirmative prayer will help to clear up old ideas that are no longer working and aid in their release.

## How to Pray Affirmatively

There are several key components to an affirmative prayer. First and foremost, the prayer must be aligned with Spirit. Working with Spirit toward a goal that is not aligned with Spirit will ultimately create frustration and failure. Ensuring alignment with Spirit is quite simple and can be done with two simple questions.

The first of these questions is: Does this harm anybody or anything? Anything you may be seeking that includes harm is not aligned spiritually and should be abandoned immediately. Remember that everything is interconnected. Praying for harm done to anybody or anything will result in harm for you. The desire for harm gets dropped into your consciousness bucket and must be accounted for. If your desire results either directly or indirectly in harm of any kind, reframe it immediately.

Beware of prayers for "justice" as there is often an underlying urge for vengeance. Remember, everybody is subject to their own consciousness bucket and true justice will always be done through the balancing of that bucket. From the spiritual perspective, justice is not our responsibility.

The second question to consider is: Do I desire this same thing for everybody? If the answer is "no," then your desire is not spiritually aligned and should not be brought to your prayer practice.

We are all connected through the omnipresence of Spirit. To want something for yourself alone or for just a select few is not aligned with Spirit because Spirit encompasses everybody, and as such, Spirit cannot provide something to one person without it being available to all people.

To put it another way, if you want something, obviously you feel that what you want is "good." If you want this "good" only for yourself, then included in your desire is the intention to withhold "good" from others. Is not withholding "good" from others harmful?

As long as a desire does not harm anybody or anything and you want your desire for everybody in addition to yourself, then it is spiritually aligned and is appropriate to bring to affirmative prayer. Anything, from the mundane to the magnificent, which fits these qualifications, is fair game.

Do you want a wonderful parking place to be waiting for you when you pull up to the grocery store? Having said parking space certainly doesn't harm anybody. Wouldn't it be wonderful for everybody to have excellent and easy parking? Yes! So pray for parking spaces if you feel so inclined.

Do you want to win the lottery? Does anybody get harmed if you win the lottery? No. Would you love for anybody to win the lottery also – that means anybody, even the bully from elementary school? If so, pray for the lottery!

It is important to note that while one of the qualifications of an aligned prayer is that you would want your desire for everybody, praying for specific things for other people without their express request or permission is strongly discouraged. Without such consent you cannot be sure that somebody else wants what you are praying for. It is absolutely okay to pray for people who request prayer. It is even okay to pray generically for somebody's "highest good," without their request. However, any specificity in prayer for others must be left up to them to determine.

## Spiritual Mind Treatment

While affirmative prayer can take on any form, Centers for Spiritual Living teaches a very powerful form of affirmative prayer called Spiritual Mind Treatment, or just Treatment. This form of prayer has five steps that provide an excellent framework. The five steps of Treatment are: Recognition, Unification, Realization, Thanksgiving, and Release. Of course, these steps come after determining what the Treatment is to be about and assuring that it's spiritually aligned. After exploring each step, an example of a Treatment will follow.

The **Recognition** step of Treatment is to recognize the presence of God or Spirit as all there is. The person praying will also call forth the qualities of Spirit that are directly related to what is being prayed for. If the prayer is for health, recognition that God is complete and perfect health, wholeness, and well-being would be called forth in this step. Recognition is perhaps the most important step in Treatment as it sets the tone for the rest of the prayer. The more complete the Recognition, the easier the rest of the Treatment will flow.

In the **Unification** step, the person praying unifies him or herself with God. We are all inseparably part of Spirit, whether we consciously recognize it or not. This step is about bringing your conscious awareness to that oneness. The qualities of Spirit that were listed in Recognition are reiterated in Unification as being true of the person praying as one with God.

**Realization** speaks to the purpose of the prayer or the thing or experience that is desired. What is desired is described in detail as a present reality. If health is being prayed for, the Realization step expresses what that health looks and feels like and claims it as presently in the experience of the person praying. This is the affirmative piece of the prayer. What is desired is claimed as already done.

From the Realization that what has been prayed for already is, the person praying moves into **Thanksgiving**, or expressing gratitude for the fulfillment of the prayer.

To finish the Treatment, it is **Released** as a whole, complete, and perfect "work" into the Universe. The Treatment itself is considered an accomplished *thing* that, having been released, goes about expressing itself in the experience of the person praying. In this step, the individual also releases any attachment to the outcome of the prayer and any doubts, fears or worries.

The following, italicized text is an example of a Treatment. The purpose of this treatment is for the experience of greater financial abundance. Each step is labeled.

*Recognition:* There is only one Life, one Presence, and one Power. This Life is perfect, it is the perfect Life of God and it is my life. Being all that there is, this Life is all abundance, all prosperity, and all wealth. It is overflowing goodness in every way, shape and form. This Life gives completely of Itself to Itself and is completely open and accepting in its receiving. This Life is *ALL THERE IS.*

*Unification:* As this Life is all there is, it must therefore be the Life I live. I am one with the Life of Spirit, immersed, enmeshed, and unextractably connected to It. What Spirit is, I Am. The abundance of Spirit is my abundance. The prosperity of Spirit is my prosperity. The wealth of Spirit is my wealth. Since God is all there is, there can be nothing other, and God and I are united as one.

*Realization:* I am one with the source of all wealth. I am one with the idea and the concept of wealth itself. Unlimited abundance flows from the source of all abundance, God, to me as an interconnected expression of God. I am already one with the source of all abundance, prosperity and wealth and therefore one with prosperity, abundance, and wealth itself.

I now open and receive more powerfully, more fully, more completely of the abundance, prosperity, and wealth that God is and I am. I release and cancel any beliefs in lack or limitation, for God is all there is and God is unlimited good. God is the ONLY source of my good and God has limitless avenues through which to deliver my good to me and I receive from ALL OF THEM!

*This new and greater experience of the limitless wealth that is who and what I am, brings with it significantly more grace as I move through the world. Money loves me! Money can't help but find its way to me. I am abundantly wealthy NOW and I experience an overflow of wealth in every area of my life. All of my financial obligations are easily met and after my financial obligations are all met, I have more and more and more money and wealth to share, and through which I experience constant luxury!*

***Thanksgiving:*** *I am so grateful! I am overflowing with gratitude for the truth of this Treatment. I am blessed beyond measure by the speaking of this prayer. My overwhelming gratitude flows from my every pore and floats my every experience to greater and greater heights of exultation. Thank you, God! Thank you, Spirit! Thank you, Life!*

***Release:*** *It is done. It is perfect. I release all doubt, all worry, all fear. This treatment is whole, complete and perfect. It is energetically infused with Life and is unstoppable in its expression in my life. All of this, or something EVEN BETTER for the Highest Good of all concerned is already done. And so it is!*

This form of prayer may feel long and awkward. And it is, at first. But over time and with practice, this format will become second nature. There are a few keys to speed up the process of getting this way of praying to feel more natural. The first of these is to **write out the prayer**. Beginning with the purpose of the prayer, writing by hand or typing the prayer will help you keep the order of the steps straight until they are memorized. Once written, reading the prayer out loud is the next step. This takes the prayer from the intellectual side of writing it down, or crafting it, and brings it to life.

Secondly, it is beneficial whenever possible to pray out loud. Speaking a prayer, rather than thinking it, helps to energize it. Not only is there the thought-form of the prayer in your mind, but your vocal energy is added to the prayer when it is spoken out loud.

## The Two Components of the Prayer

There are basically two components to the prayer; form and feeling. The first of these is the *form*. The words and the thoughts behind those words are the form of the prayer, or the body of the prayer. Frankenstein's monster is an oddly perfect metaphor for this.

When you write, think, and speak a prayer, you are creating the body of the prayer by stitching it together piece by piece. If you stop there, you have nothing but an inanimate body. What is still needed is the electricity. The *feeling* and emotion you put into the prayer is like the lightning bolt that jolted Frankenstein's monster to life.

Luckily, the metaphor ends there. Your prayers will not go about accidently killing peasants and inciting angry, torch-wielding mobs. But in order for your prayer to be as effective as possible, it must be energized with your emotions and energy! The more enthusiastically you speak your prayer, the more energized it will be. The more certainty you put behind the words, the more metaphysical weight they will carry.

Remember that consciousness bucket? Each prayer you speak goes into that bucket. A prayer spoken with boredom and disbelief will do little in your consciousness bucket. A prayer spoken with zeal and certainty will go much farther in altering the balance of the bucket. Furthermore, the more often you practice this form of prayer, the greater your consciousness will be conditioned to recognize all prayer as affirmative.

This is very important because you may find yourself in a circumstance where there isn't the time to formulate a Five-step Spiritual Mind Treatment and speak it out loud. However, the more attuned your consciousness of prayer is toward affirmative prayer, the better significantly shorter prayers will work in a pinch.

Many years ago I was in just such a pinch. My roommate was moving to London, I couldn't afford the townhouse we were sharing on my own, and I didn't know anybody else I would be willing to have as a roommate. I needed to find a new place to live and I had a hard deadline. I looked and I looked and I wasn't finding anything, and the deadline was getting very, very close. I was at work, doing my best to look for new places to live and not having any luck. I was stressed because I was facing not having a home. I was stressed because I wanted to look for a new place but was at work and knew I was supposed to be focusing on my job. My stress built and built until, fully exasperated, I said, "God help me!"

In that exact moment, the power in the building went down. I was now unable to do my work, because there was no power, and I was unable to look for a new place to live for the same reason. All of that stress disappeared in that moment. The next day I went online and found the perfect new place to live.

But wait, there's more! It turns out that the reason the power went out is that a Department of Water and Power technician cut the wrong wire, which also shut down the power to about half of Los Angeles. The apartment I found was supposed to have been rented out on the day the power was cut, but because there was no power, credit checks could not be run and that potential tenant didn't show back up later to complete the process. Not only did the power outage take away my moment of stressful overload, but it assured that the apartment I eventually moved into would still be available for me.

All of that synchronicity did not result from a five-step affirmative prayer, spoken with enthusiasm and confidence. It resulted from three words spoken from a place of utter desperation. However, that short and desperate prayer was filtered through a consciousness steeped in spiritual principles and so carried the energy and intention of a five-step affirmative prayer spoken with enthusiasm and confidence. The more you practice and condition your consciousness to affirmative prayer when there is the space to do so, the more that energy will carry any prayer.

## This or Something Better...

There is another component that is very important to include in every prayer and that is the phrase, "...this or something even better, for the Highest Good of all concerned." Have you ever wished for something you didn't get, but looking back on it you are grateful your wish was never fulfilled? That is precisely the reason for including this phrase in every prayer.

You may pray for something truly believing it is for your highest good, but lack a critical piece of information that would change your mind about what you want. Spirit has that critical information. Spirit, being omniscient or all knowing, has all the information. Including "this or something better" allows for that Universal Intelligence to expand our vision. But to make it even simpler than that, allowing for "this or something better" leaves room in our vision for more than we can imagine.

For years, I wanted to skydive. I thought about it. I imagined it. I daydreamed about what it would be like to be completely in the grip of gravity, feeling more like I was flying than falling. For my 29th birthday I decided it was time to actually go for it. My imaginations about how amazing of an experience I would have were nowhere close to how amazing it actually was. If my prayer had been for just what I thought skydiving would be, I would have missed out.

This is true in much greater depth, clarity, and intensity with my wife. When I prayed to meet and fall in love with the woman of my dreams, I left it open for Spirit to deliver more than I could possibly imagine. And that is exactly what happened. The best I could imagine was a candle flame in the distance. Spirit delivered the Sun. Our best imaginings are paltry things compared to what the Universe has in store for us, but it will deliver only our best imaginings if we don't leave room for "this or something even better."

## Connecting to Spirit

Affirmative prayer is a vital component of a robust spiritual practice. What we are looking for from a spiritual practice is a greater experience of our connection to Spirit, and affirmative prayer certainly does that. Every time you enter into prayer you attune your consciousness to Spirit. This is the first step in affirmative prayer. You then align yourself with Spirit. Step one and step two can be summed up with, "God is all there is, I Am that." If God is all there is, and I can identify myself as being that, then there is nothing other for me to be but an integral and connected part of

God. The more you go through step one and step two, the more your consciousness of connection to Spirit deepens.

The more you recognize your connection to Spirit and the deeper you understand and embody what being connected to God, as a piece of God, means, the richer life becomes. This connection can take a tree and turn it into a gift just for you. This connection can cause what others view as coincidence to be an overwhelming experience of gratitude as an example of Spirit at work in your life.

Wealth has nothing to do with money. People with little money can feel wealthy and somebody with billions of dollars can feel poor. True wealth comes from this connection to Spirit and your experience of it.

The practice of affirmative prayer also helps to build up your power of faith. I have manifested parking spaces many, many times. These days it is much more likely than not that I will get a parking space pretty easily, even in crowded parking lots where others have trouble.

While the parking spaces are wonderful and I am grateful for my skill at manifesting them through affirmative prayer, they are really only the icing on the cake. The real reward is the recognition that my prayers are indeed answered. Every time a parking place shows up, I have another example in my consciousness bucket that God does indeed hear me.

Every successful prayer builds your confidence in your ability to pray successfully. In the beginning it could be easy to feel discouraged, as it may seem like your prayers don't work very well or very often. That was certainly my experience. But over time, with practice, I began to notice more and more prayers being answered. The more I noticed my success in simpler things, like parking spaces, the more it seemed complex things, like needing a new car or a place to live, would work out miraculously.

Prayer is a skill and just like any other skill, the more you practice the better you become. If there are big things in your life needing prayer, pray for big things. If there are small things, pray for those. Just pray. Practice.

## Receiving

There is another key component to prayer work and that is receiving. The Universe is an affirmative Universe. It always answers "Yes." Yet, often times the answer to your prayers will appear to be "No." In such cases there are four possible culprits. Firstly, your prayer may not be aligned with the way Spirit works. If your prayer harbors any ill will toward anybody else, expect it to fail. Secondly, that for which you are praying might not be for your Highest good. The third possibility is that it may be that the manifestation of your prayer is taking longer than you expected. Lastly, you may be praying for something that is beyond your current ability to receive.

Imagine somebody who has a hard time allowing other people to pay for lunch without feeling guilty praying for $100,000. Their difficulty accepting a $10 lunch is a pretty strong indicator that they won't be able to accept 10,000 times the cost of a lunch.

Sure, if somebody were to walk up to them and offer them the money, they might well accept it, but their difficulty receiving far less than what they pray for will more likely than not kill their prayer before it ever comes close to that. The Universe always says "Yes," but if we are not able to receive, then that "Yes" will look like a "No."

Patience is also key to receiving. Your prayers set the cosmic tumblers in motion. Locks work on a system of tumblers. The jagged edges on your keys lift the proper tumblers the proper amount and allow the lock to be opened. In the physical world lock and key metaphor, this happens in a second. In relation to manifestation however, it can take much longer. Let me share another story from my own life to highlight this.

My wife and I had been talking about moving for about a year. We had been actively looking for a few months. We were doing all of our prayer work, visualizing our ideal place, taking decisive and powerful action in the physical world, etc., but we were not finding our place. Despite not having a subscription to one of the largest apartment rental sites in Los Angeles, my wife decided to look there and see what she could find.

As it turns out, she found a duplex right in the heart of the neighborhood we wanted. Without a subscription however, there was no way to contact the owner...except that somehow the owner had managed to include their phone number (which should have been removed prior to posting, but wasn't) into the ad. Very excited, we called and set an appointment to look at the place... and it was too small. We chose to let it go.

Several months later, another ad appeared for the same duplex but for the larger unit. The owner of the duplex, who was originally living in the back unit, had purchased another house and was moving. On an intuition after looking at the first unit, my wife decided to keep the phone number, which had not been posted in the ad this time.

We were planning on calling over the weekend, but a series of events with a current neighbor, drunk and breaking a window to get into her apartment, inspired us to call that night instead. The unit was still available, but another couple had already come and put in an application. However, since we had looked at the front unit several months earlier, the owner would give us first dibs, if we came the next morning to look at the unit. We did. It was perfect. We took it.

From our first intention to move, it took almost a year. From the time we began seeking in earnest a new place to live, it took about six months. It took so long not because the prayer work we were doing was ineffective, but because so much in the physical world had to shift. My wife was inspired to look on the subscription site at the right time – one cosmic tumbler in place. The owner's phone number slipped through the system and made it into the ad – two cosmic tumblers in place. My wife was inspired to keep the phone number – three cosmic tumblers in place. The owner of the duplex had to go through the entire process of looking for and buying another house – four cosmic tumblers in place. My wife was inspired to look on the subscription site again, at the perfect time – five cosmic tumblers in place. The circumstances with our neighbor happened, urging us to call earlier than we had planned – six cosmic tumblers in place. The owner of the duplex remembered us from months earlier – seven cosmic tumblers in place, and the door unlocked.

We could have settled for any number of places we looked at in the time between beginning our search and finding the place we did. We could have assumed that our prayers had failed, just given up on a perfect place, and gone with a "close enough" place. But we didn't. We allowed the Universe time to shift everything that needed to be shifted in order for the perfect place to be available for us. And, when looking back at all that had to happen, six months was actually pretty quick!

## How Prayer Helps Bring Complete Emancipation from All Discord of Every Nature

By helping to bring you into alignment with the experiences you're seeking, prayer shifts discord into harmony. For prayer to be effective, it must be filled with energy and positive emotion. This energy and emotion can only be experienced when you create them in your body. The more you create these experiences, which are 180 degrees from discord, the more attuned you will become to them, thus calling them into your experience more and more.

Prayer also helps to build your awareness of your connection to Spirit. There is no discord in Spirit and, since you are part of Spirit, there is the potential for no discord in your experience as well. As you practice attuning to the perfection of Spirit, your connecting link to Spirit becomes clearer and the harmony that is Spirit flows into your experience much more powerfully and easily.

### Treatment regarding Affirmative Prayer

**Recognition:** *Right here, right now. Everywhere and every moment. God, Spirit, the Universe, Unconditional Love is all there is. It is present in each and every word of this prayer and is in fact the inspiration and source of every word of this prayer. God, Spirit, the Universe, Unconditional Love is the only Life there is. There is just this one Life and it is perfect.*

**Unification:** *I am. I Am. As God is, so too I Am. This life of Spirit is the only life there is and it must then be the life I live. As such, all the inspiration, creativity, enthusiasm, wisdom,* *everything that is needed to effectively and powerfully use affirmative prayer is right where I am.*

***Realization:*** *The Universe is affirmative. It is ever expanding and so seeks expansion in all life, including me. This expansion comes through my spiritual practice, including affirmative prayer. Beginning right where I am, I now enter into a practice of affirmative prayer. The whole of the Universe supports me in my efforts as I must expand for the Universe to expand. Inspiration flows through my thoughts, infusing all of my prayers with the right and perfect words. Enthusiasm spills forth from me as I practice and that energy carries my prayers forward to successful manifestation.*

*Affirmative prayer is natural and easy for me. It flows from me. I allow the words of my prayer to form the mold of my desire, and my energy and excitement and gratitude give it life! The Universe always hears my prayers. The Universe always says yes and I am always fully open and excited to receive that for which I pray.*

*I only pray for that which I desire for everybody and, as such, all of my affirmative prayers are aligned and harmonized with Spirit. No matter the words or the form of my prayer, my intention is always for the Highest Good of all concerned and, as such, I open my awareness to receive something even better than that for which I pray. I recognize that Spirit knows far better than I do what is for my Highest Good and I allow the Universe to bring me a greater blessing than I could possibly imagine! I allow the time and the space for my prayer to manifest, trusting the Universe to bring everything about in divine right and perfect timing.*

*I am powerful in my prayer and my prayers go forth, blessing all.*

***Thanksgiving:*** *Overflowing with gratitude for the "Yes!" that has already been given, I express my thanks. Knowing the limitless giving nature of Spirit warms every fiber of my being. Thank you, God. Thank you, Universe. Thank you, Spirit.*

***Release:*** *It is done. The word has been spoken, the prayer has been energized, and the answer was "Yes" from the beginning. I now release this prayer into the Universe, knowing its manifestation is already complete. All of this or something even better for the Highest Good of all concerned is already done. And so it is!*

# Chapter Nine

## Spritual Practice: Affirmations

*I*f affirmative prayer were a marathon, affirmations would be a sprint. Affirmations provide a very quick and easy way for us to make many small deposits into our consciousness bucket. An affirmation is a very short statement of Truth about something you are seeking a greater experience of in your life. It helps to pull your focus back to the positive and form new patterns of thinking. Through the use of affirmations you can recondition your mind to think in supportive ways, rather than the habitual, destructive thought patterns common in the human experience.

The only reason we tend to have the same or similar thoughts over and over again is because we have had the same or similar thoughts over and over again. Just like water following the same path for eons will erode rock into the Grand Canyon, so too do your repeated thought patterns make "grooves" in your consciousness. The more you think a thought, the easier thinking that same thought becomes. Until you become aware of this, it is far too easy to let negative thoughts carve deep grooves so that they seem to spin themselves up into your awareness all on their own. Affirmations are a powerful tool for counteracting those negative thought patterns and replacing those deep grooves of negative thinking with even deeper grooves of positive thinking.

As with all of your spiritual tools, the use of affirmations will tend to bring up old thoughts and beliefs that have been keeping you stuck. The more you recite an affirmation related to heath, the more your habitual thought patterns around health will begin to surface. This is fantastic news! By becoming aware of previously hidden beliefs, you can replace them with more accurate and beneficial beliefs.

For example, a hidden belief that doctors cause pain, based on an experience of shots as a kid, may result in a stress response every time a doctor is visited. This stress response could show up as elevated blood pressure. By becoming aware of the hidden belief and correcting it, this example of elevated blood pressure could also be corrected.

Crafting affirmations takes some care but is generally pretty simple and fun. There are very few guidelines and with a bit of practice, crafting affirmations can happen very quickly.

1. Keep it short. Affirmations should be no longer than two sentences, but one is better. The reason for this is that you want to be able to remember it exactly and repeat it easily and often the exact same way. This word-for-word repetition will help to build those consciousness grooves mentioned earlier. Keeping it short can be the most difficult of the guidelines because it requires honing the affirmation down to its core essence.

2. Keep it in present tense. Affirmations, like affirmative prayer, are to be crafted in the present tense. An affirmation would not say "I will be experiencing _____," but rather something like "I am experiencing _____ daily." The reason for this is two-fold. First, this helps to bring up

the hidden "stuff" that has been getting in the way of you experiencing _____ in the first place. If the affirmation speaks of the future, then the hidden belief has nothing to argue with and will stay hidden. If the affirmation is stated in the present – "I am abundantly wealthy NOW!" – you may notice a thought similar to "No I'm not, because I'm not good enough to be wealthy." BAM! The hidden belief has fallen for the trap, revealed itself, and can now be consciously addressed.

The second reason is that affirming something in the future keeps it in the future. If you affirm over and over again "I will be in complete health soon," then the message received by your consciousness and the Universe is "I am not now in complete health." When is it? Now. When will it be when it is tomorrow at 9:30 a.m.? Now. It is always now. If your affirmation puts your desire anywhere other than now, it will never come into now.

3. Use words that are exciting and powerful to you. The affirmation must ignite passion and belief in you when you recite it. If the words of your affirmations aren't powerful and meaningful to you, then it doesn't really matter what other people might think about them. The words "courageous" and "brave" can mean basically the same thing. But if courageous is tied in my mind to cowardly and brave relates to being empowered, then, clearly, my affirmation should use the word brave.

As long as your affirmations follow those three guidelines, they should be simple and powerful. Keep it short. Keep it present. Use words you find powerful.

## Create Your Own Affirmation Exercise

Let's take a moment to craft an affirmation that you can use right away.

1. Pick an area of your life in which you would like your experience to be different.

2. How do you want your experience of this area of your life to be? Write several sentences to a paragraph of detailed description.

3. Boil your paragraph down to one phrase that, for you, feels like a very powerful description of the experience you are looking to have.

4. Finesse your phrase into a sentence that begins with "I Am..."

5. Make any necessary adjustments to ensure that your sentence is in the present tense and short, yet powerful.

One of my favorite affirmations that I use quite often is related to health. "I Am complete, perfect, radiant, vibrant, dynamic health!" Though it is only one sentence long, this affirmation is just a bit of a mouthful. Eliminating two of the five descriptors would probably bring it down to bite-size. Another affirmation I use frequently around health is, "Wholeness is my name and nature." This particular affirmation is an excellent example of why using words that are exciting and powerful to you is so important.

"Wholeness" in my affirmation can mean a lot of different things. For me, the idea of "wholeness" encompasses a great deal more than the word itself suggests.

If something is whole that means it is not missing anything. It is complete. It is perfect. In relation to health, wholeness to me relates to my bones, muscles, joints, organs, immune system, all of it – the whole thing. Wholeness to me also relates to holy or divine. In the simple word "wholeness" my consciousness hears complete, whole, perfect health on every level in every system and function of my life anchored by and in Spirit.

"My name" also carries great weight. What is in a name? My name is how I identify myself. My name is how other people identify me. My name is how I am known in the world. I am so attuned to my name that I will turn toward a voice that I do not recognize in a crowded room full of noise if that voice says, "Hey Ben," even though it is not meant for me. It is automatic. It takes no time, no thought, and no effort for my awareness to reference myself when I hear the name Ben. Related to my affirmation, it affirms that everything wholeness means to me is how I identify myself and how others identify me. It means that everything wholeness means to me is how I view myself by default.

"My nature" adds even more depth to the affirmation. Imagine water. What is the nature of water? Water is wet. Water flows downhill. Water seeks the path of least resistance. Water freezes at 32 degrees and boils at 212 degrees. These aspects of the nature of water are constants. Nobody ever ponders, "I wonder if this water will run uphill today instead?" If wholeness is my nature it means that wholeness is the truth about me always. It means that nobody would ever even begin to consider the idea of the possibility that I am anything other than everything that wholeness means to me.

"Wholeness is my name and nature" is six words long. The three paragraph description of what it means in my awareness is 347 words, and it could have been much longer. Using words that are powerful and meaningful to you means that your few words will carry the weight of hundreds.

## How to Use Affirmations

Once an affirmation is crafted it is time to begin using it. There are two primary ways to use affirmations, proactively and responsively. No matter whether proactive or responsive, there are a few keys to get the most out of the affirmation.

Ideally, the affirmation will be spoken out loud. Speaking an affirmation, much like speaking an affirmative prayer, helps to ensure the proper feeling and energy behind the affirmation. It also, and this is true for affirmative prayer as well, helps to get it into your consciousness a bit deeper.

If an affirmation is thought, it is thought. In order for an affirmation to be spoken, it must also be thought. Additionally, by speaking an affirmation out loud it is heard and the body feels the affirmation as well through the movement of the lips and tongue. Thinking an affirmation has one entry point. Speaking it has four. Of course, it is not always appropriate to speak an affirmation out loud and thinking it is certainly better than not using it at all.

Another key to using affirmations is to feel them. Speaking or thinking an affirmation should have a visceral response. Your body or your energy should react to it in a positive way. Throw as much certainty, clarity, gratitude, and power behind your affirmations as possible.

Remember back to *Return of the Jedi* near the end of the film. (If you have not seen the original Episodes IV, V, and VI *Star Wars* films, make a point of it. And, spoiler alert!) Luke has just defeated Darth Vader and the Emperor is encouraging him to kill Darth. What does Luke say? "You have failed, Your Highness. I am a Jedi, like my father before me." I can hear the way Luke says that line. His words are soft, yet there is not a shred of doubt. He is completely confident and does not hesitate.

Now imagine how that line would have gone over if he was bored by it. Imagine if he had no confidence or commitment to what he said. He was so clear and powerful in what he said that the Emperor gave up all hope of converting Luke to the dark side. This is the clarity, power, confidence, and feeling that we need to bring to our affirmation work.

It can be easy to confuse speaking powerfully with speaking loudly. The same line of Luke's is a perfect example for this as well. "I am a Jedi, like my father before me," was not shouted or screamed. It was spoken almost a little quieter than a normal volume, yet it was infused with incredible power. Extra vocal energy can certainly help in infusing an affirmation with power, but just because something is spoken loudly does not mean that it carries anything more than decibels, and just because something is said softly does not indicate that there is no conviction behind the words.

Repetition is the third key to using affirmations. Affirmations are short and sweet because they are meant to be said often. The affirmation "Wholeness is my name and nature" can be repeated with feeling, certainty, clarity, and power many times in one minute. Each repetition is another small deposit into the bucket of "health consciousness." Individually, these deposits make little difference, but stack them up many times a day, perhaps 30, and maintain that practice every day and you have 900 deposits in one month and that is significant.

However, beware of the trap of vain repetition. "But when ye pray, use not vain repetitions, as the Gentiles do: for they think that they shall be heard for their much speaking." Matthew 6:7. Ignore the word "Gentiles" in that passage. Repetition of affirmations can easily become vain repetition, where a goal is set for one hundred repetitions of an affirmation and those repetitions are said with as much speed and as little feeling as possible, just to get the correct number of tally marks on a tracking sheet. Not only will using affirmations in vain repetition not work, it will actually be counterproductive.

Imagine an individual who wants to experience greater health. They take the affirmation "Wholeness is my name and nature" and plan to repeat it 100 times a day for 30 days and see what happens. Instead of really exploring what the affirmation means, they decide to use it because they have heard that it's a good affirmation. When it comes time to do their repetitions they think, "Dang! 100 times is a lot. I don't have that much time. Well, I'll just see how long it really takes..." They take the biggest breath they can and...

> "wholeness is my name and nature wholeness is my name and nature wholeness is my name and nature wholeness is my name and nature wholeness is my name and nature..."

By the end of it, they are out of breath, but managed to recite the affirmation one hundred times in about two minutes, but with zero belief, zero feeling, and zero commitment to anything other than reciting a sentence one hundred times as fast as possible.

After their 30-day experiment, they have recited their affirmation 3,000 times. Of course, because their only intention in their affirmation practice was on speed, if there is any difference in their experience of health at all, it is very slight. The logical next thought is, "I said this thing 3,000 times and it didn't do anything. This affirmation crap doesn't work!"

Don't believe that you will be heard for your "much speaking." The words of an affirmation are very important, but the feeling behind the affirmation is what really makes it work. One repetition of an affirmation, said with enthusiasm, belief, clarity, and certainty is far more effective than the same affirmation repeated 100 times in vain repetition.

Whenever possible, speak your affirmations out loud, infuse them with feeling, and repeat them often with the intention of making each repetition more powerful than the repetition before and your affirmation practice will bring great results.

## Proactive Use of Affirmations

Earlier, I mentioned that affirmations can be used proactively or responsively. The proactive use of affirmations involves setting a specific practice around your affirmation. Reciting an affirmation 100 times each day as part of your morning routine is a perfect example of a proactive use of affirmations.

For example, imagine that there is an experience in your life that you want to change. You craft an affirmation for what you want your experience to be. You commit to reciting that affirmation 100 times each day for 30 days and tracking your experiences along the way.

At the end of those 30 days, you assess the results and decide on your next course of action. Do you continue with the same affirmation for the next 30 days? Do you adjust the affirmation? Are there actions you need to take? Have you achieved the experience you desired?

The use of a proactive affirmation plan can provide powerful results. Over the course of time the affirmation will become more and more a part of who you are. At first, it may take a good deal of effort to get the proper feeling behind your recitations and it may take you a long while to get them all in. Over time, it will become more second nature to infuse the affirmation with feeling and power. Eventually, you will likely notice the affirmation popping into your mind at different points throughout the day, seemingly of its own accord.

## Responsive Use of Affirmations

The responsive use of affirmations happens in reply to a thought or experience. A wonderful opportunity to practice responsive affirmations happens every single year. It is called "flu season." Every year, right around the same time, "flu season" hits. Suddenly, everybody is talking about the flu, or getting the flu, or getting flu shots, or knows somebody who has the flu and it is *just terrible!*

Every time you come into contact with one of these experiences, if you aren't vigilant, it gets deposited into your health consciousness bucket and the probability of your getting the flu increases. When you understand how consciousness works, it is no wonder that so many people experience the flu during "flu season" when the news, advertisements, and everybody around us is unconsciously throwing around "flu deposits" for any health consciousness bucket that isn't equipped with a filter.

A responsive affirmation practice can be that perfect filter. In this example, every time the awareness of the flu pops into your experience, whether from the media, overheard in somebody else's conversation, or a conversation in which you are directly involved, repeat "Wholeness is my name and nature" five times. Of course, if you are directly involved in the conversation, it is best for this affirmation to be done silently.

Whether said out loud or silently, these five repetitions must not be delayed but done immediately upon noticing the flu-like input. This will not only help to filter any of the flu talk from getting into your consciousness but, if any does, will help to counteract it. This, of course, doesn't guarantee that you won't get the flu, but will help to increase the probability that you remain healthy.

This holds true of any experience. If you are working on abundance, then every time you notice a thought pop into your head that is negative toward wealth or wealthy people, counter it powerfully with five (or more) repetitions of an affirmation. This responsive use of affirmations works in a couple of ways.

Not all thoughts are created equal. Thoughts that enter our awareness from outside, such as the news or in conversation with others, weigh less in consciousness terms than thoughts that pop up in our own heads. Whether the thought is provided from outside, or simply pops into our awareness, we are responsible for what we do with it. If we then accept those thoughts as true, more weight is added to them. If we let our imaginations run wild with those thoughts and fantasize about them, we add even more weight.

However, the most powerful thoughts are those that are consciously and purposefully chosen. A lot of intention goes into crafting an affirmation. Even more consciousness and purpose are thrown behind that affirmation when we create a specific practice with it. The difference in weighting between a news media idea floating in the air and an affirmation is significant.

Imagine a volleyball. Somebody gently tosses that ball toward the volleyball net. As the ball floats through the air and is about to cross the net, a 6'5", 225-pound professional men's volleyball player jumps up and, with every bit of his finely honed skill and force, spikes the ball into the ground before it crosses the net.

This is similar to the difference between somebody else's idea floated in conversation and your counter-affirmation. Say the affirmation five times and now there are five of those professional spikers on your side of the net! This analogy is the potential result for one who puts in the time to develop the tool of affirmations.

Affirmations also work by conditioning responses in your awareness. Just like Pavlov was able to condition his dogs to salivate at the ringing of the bell, so too can you condition your awareness to respond in certain ways to certain ideas. Eventually, your responsive affirmation practice will become automatic.

After a time of responding with "Wholeness is my name and nature" to thoughts of illness, you may find "Wholeness is my name and nature" running through your mind as you flip past a pharmaceutical ad in a magazine.

There are countless examples in our society of thoughts of sickness permeating the atmosphere. By conditioning your mind to respond to every one of them with an affirmation of health, through a responsive affirmation practice, you're taking great steps to ensure your constant experience of health, regardless of what is happening around you.

## Keeping Thoughts out, Not Suppressing Thoughts Already in

Keep in mind, the purpose of a responsive affirmation practice is to build the consciousness of what you do want, not to suppress that which you do not want. Keeping outside thoughts from getting into your consciousness is one thing, but suppressing thoughts that are already there is not helpful.

When a thought comes into your awareness that is counter to what you want to experience, it is absolutely appropriate to apply a responsive affirmation practice, but only to build the consciousness of what you want. The thoughts that surface from your own subconscious must be dealt with differently, through forgiveness.

Through forgiveness, you can release and clear these old beliefs rather than shoving them back down. Forgiveness will be discussed in detail later. For now, just be sure, when using responsive affirmations in relation to thoughts clearly originating within your own being, you are not shoving them back down and refusing to look at what is already present within you.

## Using Both Proactive and Responsive Affirmations

Proactive and responsive affirmation practices go hand in hand. If you are establishing a proactive affirmation practice to experience more love in your life, then you will begin to notice more often when thoughts pop up in your awareness that are blocking your experience of love, or when you see things or hear ideas that are not supportive of loving. When such thoughts or experiences do enter your awareness, using the same affirmation that is involved in your proactive practice, counter them with your responsive practice. While a responsive practice can be implemented independently of any proactive process, a proactive process necessitates a responsive counterpart.

## Thought Grooves

If you do not already notice certain patterns of thought that tend to repeat themselves over and over again as you engage in establishing a spiritual practice, and in particular using affirmations, you will. In my own experience, the responsive affirmation practice has been vital in overcoming these repeating thought patterns.

Many years ago, I began to notice how frequently, when I was driving, thoughts about accidents happening either to me or around me would pop into my awareness. As soon as I noticed this pattern, I set about to change it. Remember, all thoughts are deposits into our consciousness bucket and the more deposits we make of a certain thought, the more probable that thought manifesting becomes.

Clearly, I do not want to experience auto accidents and so I knew I needed to stop these thoughts from popping up. But why were they popping up in the first place? The answer is something I refer to as thought grooves.

The more you engage in a certain type of thinking, the more your consciousness becomes trained to think those thoughts. It is almost like a thought groove or pathway is formed and when unformed thought energy is released, if not consciously directed, it will follow the path of least resistance, or the deepest groove.

Imagine a smooth field filled with long, wavy, waist-high grass. You walk a path through that field, bending the grasses underfoot as you do. The more you walk that same path, the more trampled the grasses become. Eventually, your path has been walked so many times there is no longer any grass, just a dirt trail. Now, without significant effort on your part, you will follow that same path through, every time. It is often said that humans have about 50,000 thoughts a day and that most of these are reruns.

Now, imagine that you have realized that there is a much better way through the field and you want to change your path. This will be difficult because there is waist-high grass everywhere in the field except on the path you have walked for so long. You know your old path so well, that even though you desire a new path, you walk the old one out of habit. Despite the difficulty, you are committed to making that new path.

You begin proactively by consciously walking through the grass along your desired new route each morning. A few days later, before you realize it, you are half way down your original path out of habit. Having caught yourself, you immediately leave the old path, cutting through the field, to where you are clearing the new trail and finish your path through the field on the new trail. This pattern continues, where you intentionally walk the new path, but occasionally catch yourself somewhere along the old path. You are catching yourself sooner and sooner and, each time, you immediately cut over to your new path.

Eventually the new path is as clear as the old path and so, as you reach the field, you have a clearer choice and choose your new path. Over time, with less and less walking along the original path, the grasses begin to regrow and there is no sign that you ever walked that way before.

Re-grooving thought patterns using affirmation works much the same way. Deeply grooved thoughts of "I'm unlovable" will carry a person over and over again until a new choice is made. Consciously affirming "I come from Love, am Love, am loving, lovable, and loved" one hundred times each morning will begin to form the new groove.

Every time the old pattern of "I'm unlovable" pops up, "I come from Love, am Love, am loving, lovable, and loved" is affirmed five times. The old thought pattern is caught quicker and easier each time it crops up.

Then one day, the awareness that the "unlovable" pattern is about to run happens just before it does, and the path of Love is chosen instead. Over time, through disuse, the thought groove of "I'm unlovable" repairs and refills itself.

This may make the use of affirmations sound difficult or heavy, but rest assured, affirmations can be easy and fun. Imagine choosing to establish an affirmation practice around health. If you hear somebody sneeze, after saying "bless you," you say (internally or externally as appropriate), "I am radiant, vibrant, dynamic health!" Every time you hear a cough, "I am radiant, vibrant, dynamic health!" In reply to every drug ad, "I am radiant, vibrant, dynamic health!" It almost becomes a game, and playing this game makes you feel great because you are bombarding yourself with these positive ideas all day long!

## How Affirmations Help Bring Complete Emancipation from all Discord of Every Nature

Remember, the goal of a spiritual practice is complete emancipation of all discord of every nature. Once again, Shakespeare reminds us that "there is nothing either good or bad, but thinking makes it so." (You may have noticed this is the third time that quote has been mentioned. This is intentional. Embodying an understanding of this idea is exceptionally important in your spiritual practice and life in general.) Discord in your experience comes not from your experiences but how you *think* about your experiences. The primary purpose of affirmations is to change and condition what and how you think. If you do not consciously condition your thinking patterns, then they will default to the lowest common thinking pattern available, which is race consciousness.

# Treatment regarding Affirmations

**Recognition:** *There is only one Life. This Life is perfect. This Life is the perfect Life of God. It is the only Presence and Power active as my life and as the Universe.*

**Unification:** *As there is only this one Life, it must be the Life that I live. Born in the image and likeness of Spirit, I Am that which Spirit is. The creative capacity of the Universe resides fully and completely within me and I use it consciously, one with the One that is All.*

**Realization:** *The Universe is an affirmative universe. As an integral and ever-connected piece of the Universe, in order for the Universe to expand I must expand. As such, the entire Universe conspires for my expansion and growth and supports me fully in all of my efforts to craft my own spiritual practice, including the powerful and effective use of affirmations.*

*The affirmations I write are divinely inspired. The right and perfect words flow from Divine Mind through me into the perfect affirmation for every occasion. My work with affirmations is joyful. I revel in the simplicity and power of their use. When I repeat my affirmations I do so with certainty, clarity, conviction, and power. Each recitation is more powerful than the one before and with each speaking of my affirmations my energy rises higher and higher.*

*Quickly and powerfully, my practice with affirmations erases patterns of thinking that no longer serve my highest good and replaces them with new thoughts, new patterns that propel me forward toward complete emancipation from all discord of every nature. My affirmations also serve as a fool-proof consciousness filter, keeping my awareness and consciousness clean, clear, and powerfully my own.*

***Thanksgiving:*** *I am so grateful for my powerfully effective practice of affirmations. Joy pours from my being. I soar on the energy of "Thank you!"*

***Release:*** *It is done! I release this prayer to the Universe, which has already received and acted upon it. Knowing that this prayer is fully aligned with Spirit, and knowing that it will be this prayer or something even better for the Highest Good, I claim it done. There is nothing else to do, save to receive and rest in appreciation of this moment now. And So It IS!*

# Chapter Ten

## Spiritual Practice: Love

$\mathcal{I}$t may seem odd at first to have love as a component of a spiritual practice. Love isn't really taught very well in our society. It often seems that society views love as something that happens to you, not necessarily something that you do. But in fact, love is a choice and love is a practice. Love is the most powerful tool available in your spiritual practice. But in order to learn to use and practice love effectively, you must first learn more about love.

A little internet research will bring up a lot of information about the different types of love (brought forward by the Greeks), but I like to look at love a little differently and categorize it into three basic types of love. You can use these ideas to practice loving. By being more loving through your practice, you have more love in your life.

### The 3 Types of Love: Impersonal Love

The first of these types of love is Impersonal love. Impersonal love refers to a love that is more generalized and all encompassing. With Impersonal love we can say to anybody "I love you" and be sincere. Impersonal love says that I love you because you exist, because I am aware of you, and for no other reason than that.

Existing is a pretty big thing, when you really think about it. What did you do to deserve existence? The answer is nothing. There is nothing anybody can "do" to deserve existence, just as there is nothing anybody can do to deserve not to exist. We exist because we are part of the interconnected whole of Spirit. Recalling the metaphor of the wave on the surface of the ocean, it would seem silly to love one wave and not another. They are all waves on the surface of the ocean.

Impersonal love is, by definition, not personal and not romantic. Impersonal love acknowledges basic, inherent value in everything and everybody, regardless of what they may have done or not done. This can be a sticking point for a lot of people, and understandably so.

Impersonal love requires that we love, on this most basic level, people who commit murder, set fires, and even the people you despise the most. The key to this is to separate the person from what they do. Notice that I did not say we must love murder, but that we must love the person regardless of their act of murder. Every act of murder must either be balanced OR be balancing something else, and it is not given to us to know which.

Let's say that Bob murders Jack. On our human level of awareness that is all we know - that Bob murdered Jack. But there is far more going on than just Bob and Jack in this incarnation. What if, in a previous incarnation Bob murdered a few people, was never caught, and from a soul-level perspective feels that the best way to balance that out is to murder somebody again, get caught, and spend the rest of that incarnation in jail. Perhaps Jack's previous incarnation saw him cause a lot of harm through corporate greed and he decides, on the soul-level, that the best way to balance that harm out is to be murdered in his next incarnation. Spirit says, "Hey Bob, meet Jack. Looks like you two could really help each other out in this next incarnation." From this perspective, Bob murdering Jack is not bad at all, but exactly what both of them felt was necessary from a higher level of awareness than we have access to.

Obviously, this example should not be read as to condone murder or any other violation of the law. The point is that there is no way for us to really know what is going on in the spiritual context of a situation. Since we don't know, any story we tell is one that has been made up. If we are going to make up stories, we might as well make up stories that support our staying at peace and spiritually centered.

When you get caught up in punishment you are thrown off of your spiritual center. Love is your spiritual center and you cannot be at the same time in an experience of love and concerned with how to punish somebody. Being concerned with punishment says that you know better than the Universe.

The Universe seeks balance, not punishment. If you feel punishment is required then you are saying that the Universe is wrong. Can the wave know better than the ocean? Can the wave have any idea what is happening in the ocean 3,000 feet below the ocean's surface?

The practice of Impersonal love is the practice of divorcing in our awareness the person from what the person does and simply loving the person. Impersonal love turns a blind eye to what people do. Impersonal love recognizes that you and I are in the same boat. We both exist! Since we exist, we must be valuable. Since we both exist, you must be as deserving of this existence as I am. You must be as deserving of love as I am. And that is the crux of the whole thing. I am deserving of love. You are deserving of love. Impersonal love establishes that love for one and all but, in your experience, only to the degree that you practice it.

If I love all people simply because they exist and recognize that their existence implies inherent value and lovability, then I must include myself as part of "all people." Recognizing inherent value and lovability in others means that I too am inherently valuable and lovable. If, on the other hand, I withhold this most basic level of loving from somebody because of something they did or did not do, I am cutting myself off from love as well.

Think about it... How do you know love is present? How does anybody know love is present? You can only know love is present by experiencing it. When you practice Impersonal love, you experience love in yourself. If I withhold love from somebody, then love is not present and I do not experience love. Love emanates from us, and flows through us. When you love, that energy fills your experience. When you withhold love, your connection to love and the power it brings is cut off, by you.

## Withholding Love

Let's try an experiment. Bring to mind somebody that you love. This should be somebody who you just can't help but feel love toward whenever you are around them or they enter your mind. It could be a parent, child, partner, friend, or pet. It really doesn't matter. Bring that person to mind and just love them like you usually do. Feel the love flowing from you, through you, to them. What does it feel like in your body to just love? Explore the feelings.

Now, and without any malice, stop sending love to that person. Cut off the flow of love to them. What does it feel like in your body now? How has your experience changed?

Please, without hesitation, return to loving that person again. Allow the love to once again flow through you, to them.

How was that experience for you? For myself, in simply typing out the experiment, I felt the constriction in my body. I felt my energy drop. I felt sadness roll in to where the loving had been flowing and wanted nothing more than to re-engage the love experience. As soon as I did, "Ahhhhhhh....." My body relaxed, ease returned, and the sadness disappeared.

Now that you have had this experience of what it is like to withhold love and what it does to you, does the practice of Impersonal love seem more important?

We have countless opportunities to practice this basic kind of love and by doing so, be in the flow of that love ourselves, or to withhold love. We can decide not to recognize that, by simply being alive, everybody deserves love and with that decision cut ourselves off from love. The experience of love is healing and life-giving. Practicing Impersonal love is a great way to bring loving more readily into our lives and being good at Impersonal love is essential for practicing the other two types of love.

## The 3 Types of Love: Direct Love

The second form of love is Direct love. Direct love is the next level up of loving and happens when love becomes personal. Direct love relates to friends, family, pets, and romantic love. In order to practice Direct love, I must allow you into my experience in a personal way. Impersonal love can be practiced generally toward the entire planet. Direct love can only exist with people you actually know.

A lot of confusion comes into play with Direct love because of its personal nature. This is where our societal

113

heebie-jeebies are likely to come into play. Society is so confused about what love is that saying "I love you" to people can be stressful or interpreted as inappropriate. This comes from some very fundamental misunderstandings about love when we add the personal element to Impersonal love.

<u>Misunderstanding One:</u> Because you know somebody, you have to have Direct love for them instead of Impersonal love. Impersonal love is generic and, when practiced correctly, applies to all people regardless of whether or not we know them personally. Direct love requires a personal relationship. But just because you have a personal relationship with somebody does not mean that they automatically get counted in your Direct love circle. You get to choose who you allow into your Direct love tribe and who you do not.

It is not bad, or wrong, or mean to leave somebody in Impersonal love. I am reminded of a joke by the late Mitch Hedberg about escalators. "An escalator can never break: it can only become stairs. You should never see an Escalator Temporarily Out of Order sign, just Escalator Temporarily Stairs. Sorry for the convenience." If somebody that you know does not become part of your Direct love tribe, then you still love them anyway because everybody is included in your Impersonal love.

The people who become part of your Direct love tribe in fact should be very carefully selected. These people can have a great deal of influence in your life, and to a certain degree, Direct love requires trust and vulnerability.

Furthermore, just because somebody is currently in your Direct love circle doesn't mean that they always will be. There are plenty of people throughout my lifetime with whom I am no longer in contact. The personal aspect of my love relationship with these people is no longer in place, yet I still love them in the Impersonal sense.

Misunderstanding Two: Loving somebody who is not your family means you want to have sex with them. This misunderstanding applies particularly in relation to the gender that we are sexually attracted to. "I can't tell them I love them. If I do they might think that I'm attracted to them." Our society has the words love and sex crossed incorrectly. We think that loving somebody means you want to have sex with them, but having sex with somebody doesn't have to have anything to do with love. This is backwards. Loving somebody doesn't have to have anything to do with sex, and sex without loving present is empty.

Despite the fact that the idea of love relating to sex is false, it still exists in our society and as such we do have to navigate these waters carefully. Expressing love for your boss, even if your intention has nothing to do with romance, may well be taken incorrectly and cause you a bit of trouble in the physical world. But there is nothing to say that you cannot recognize that more personal level of loving within yourself.

There are some of my former co-workers that I love quite deeply. I love them generically through Impersonal love, but I have also come to know them well and that closeness has up-leveled my Impersonal love for these people to Direct love. In my experience, this love is deep and profound...and has absolutely nothing to do with sexuality. I would love to express this love, but a married man saying "I love you" to a female co-worker isn't commonly accepted. But I don't have to tell anybody that I love them in order to love them. I can simply love them.

Misunderstanding Three:   Because love relates to sex, it isn't okay to express love to people of genders to which you aren't sexually attracted.  This misunderstanding applies more generally to men than women, but for sure both genders have this misunderstanding to one degree or another.  This largely relates to the idea that love, outside of family and very close friends, relates to sex, which is really just silly.  I can tell a male who happens to be my brother that I love him and it doesn't relate to sex at all.  I can tell a male who's as close to me as family that I love him and it doesn't relate to sex at all.  But, if I express love for a male who is just an okay friend, it is all awkward and "gay"?  Give me a break!

When we reach Direct love, there is no "one size fits all" love.  Impersonal love is one size fits all, but every person with whom you share a Direct connection has a different quality of loving involved.  And that is okay.  Loving people is okay.  Loving co-workers is okay.  Loving people of the same gender is okay. Loving people of the opposite gender is okay.  Love is love and has nothing at all to do with sex of itself.  We are able to bring love and sex together, but love itself is just love, regardless of who it is that you are loving.

Misunderstanding Four:  Saying "I love you" requires a similar response.  The only thing you will ever get out of your loving is the experience of loving.  Too often, we use love in an attempt to get something from somebody else.  If we say "I love you" and expect the other person to say the same, we are perpetuating the problem.  The expectation of a certain response rides on our words and is picked up by the other person.

Nobody likes to feel obligated to respond in a particular way to anything.  If you give a gift with the expectation that the receiver will give you a gift as well, isn't the act of giving diminished?  The same holds true of expressing love while expecting an expression of love in return.

When we were first dating, I told my wife that I loved her before she was ready to say the same to me, and that was completely okay.  I did not tell her that I loved her to find out if she felt the same way.  I told her I loved her because my experience of loving toward her was such that I had to share it.  I shared it for me, not for her.  I am sure it was wonderful for her to hear, and I certainly wanted her to know that I loved her, but I expressed my love for her out of my love for her and for no other reason.

She told me she was not yet ready to say the same.  This was totally fine with me, but I told her that I was going to continue to say "I love you" going forward and that she should feel no obligation to say the same until she truly felt the same.

In our relationship today, we have an understanding that phone conversations are closed with mutual expressions of love and that when one of us says "I love you," the other responds in kind.  This, however, is not an unspoken assumption but rather a conscious agreement that we have made.  It is nice to hear the words "I love you" and it is nice to be validated by hearing the same back.  We have this agreement for these reasons and part of that agreement is an understanding that if I forget an "I love you" it does not mean that I don't love my wife, and that if she doesn't respond in kind, it doesn't mean that my expression of love was not received.

## The 3 Types of Love:  Unconditional Love

The final form of love is Unconditional love.  Unconditional love instantly makes the generic Impersonal love personal, bypassing (if necessary) Direct love.  It is the highest form of love and is our ultimate goal. In both Impersonal and Direct love, the possibility of withholding love exists. In Unconditional love, it does not. While Unconditional love can take a great deal of practice to achieve, it is actually our natural state of being.

Just like the wave is an inseparable part of the ocean and is what the ocean is, so too are we inseparable from God and are what God is. God is Unconditional Love and unconditionally loving. As part of God, we too are Unconditional love. Our human experience has conditioned us to forget this truth, but forgetting it doesn't make it any less true.

Unconditional love says, "I love you completely for who and what you are." This may sound similar to Impersonal love but where Impersonal love turns a blind eye to people's actions, Unconditional love sees those actions. Impersonal love says to the murderer, "I'm not going to acknowledge that you murdered somebody and love you just because you exist." Unconditional love says, "I know that you have murdered people. I love you anyway. You are so much more than what you do or what you don't do." Unconditional love is so complete and so accepting that nothing anybody does can lessen it. This does not make atrocious acts okay. Again, as with Impersonal love, Unconditional love is directed toward the person, not the person's actions.

Like Direct love, Unconditional love requires vulnerability. Unlike Direct love, it requires complete vulnerability. In Direct love we are able to meter how vulnerable we are with others. Not so with Unconditional love. However, an interesting thing happens when we love on this highest of levels. When we become completely vulnerable, we are actually no longer vulnerable at all.

If we are vulnerable, it means that we are open to being wounded. The only way we can be wounded is if we have something to protect, something that we don't want wounded. Perfect vulnerability removes all concern with protection. With nothing to protect, there is nothing to wound.

We all know the experience of dreading telling somebody who we love about something in our lives. We build it up to such a horrific thing and then finally break down and tell them. No matter how they react, our secret has lost most if not all of its charge. We can no longer be hurt by it because it is out in the open.

Unconditional love recognizes the inseparable connection between yourself and every other person. One wave is not separate from the next wave. It might look separate in form, but beyond the form the same ocean makes both waves. Loving somebody unconditionally because of the recognition that they are what you are and you are what they are, leads to the expression of Unconditional love.

Ultimately, Unconditional love means Unconditional love and acceptance of yourself. This can seem like a very daunting task, but the good news is that you have plenty of time to get there (no matter your age), and a robust spiritual practice will help.

It is interesting to recognize how much easier it is having Unconditional love for somebody else than it is to have Unconditional love for ourselves. And yet we so desperately need that Unconditional love from ourselves. You can feel it, if you feel deep enough. You can hear it, if you listen close enough. There is a place inside that says, "If only you would love me, no matter what, everything would be heaven." If only Ben would love Ben completely, no matter what Ben does or does not do, then Ben's experience would be heavenly all the time.

We can only receive that which we are willing to give to ourselves. God loves you, me, everybody, unconditionally.

But what does that matter in my experience if I cannot receive it? The more I love myself, the more love I am able to receive from others.

Everybody has had the experience of trying to compliment somebody else, but no matter what is said, the compliments are continually turned aside. Our compliments make no difference because the person is unable to receive them. How often are you the one who refuses to accept the compliment? Loving yourself unconditionally opens you to receive Unconditional love from others, and from Spirit.

Impersonal, Direct, and Unconditional love provide you with three clear steps in working up toward Unconditional love of yourself. You can begin with generically loving everybody.

Find a random stranger. Starting with a stranger is wise because, having no knowledge of the person, it is easier to begin at a neutral place inside. Observe them and think to yourself, "You exist and so you are valuable and lovable. I love you because you exist and I love myself because I exist too." Then, energetically send that person loving energy.

The very act of loving requires that you experience love as well, so recognize that the loving energy you are sending to the stranger is loving energy you are giving to yourself as well. Try it. See how you feel.

Keep practicing until you get really good with random strangers, and then, try the not so random stranger. Continue with successively more difficult circumstances until you are able to divorce anybody from their actions and love them just because they exist.

Bring this same level of love to people in your Direct love tribe, but add the sweetness of your personal connection to it. Pay attention to the differences in how your Direct love feels with different people so that you begin to notice the richness and variety. All of that richness and variety of loving experience flows through you and is yours because you notice it. As you feel comfortable, bring in vulnerability to certain of those relationships, bit by bit. Recognize as you do so, that being vulnerable with others means you are more vulnerable with yourself as well. Pay attention, over time, to how the Direct love grows as you open to more vulnerability and connection.

When it comes to Unconditional love, start where it is easy! Pets are great. Babies are great. Do your very best to see them as clearly as you can. See *them*, not what you think about them. This is easiest when they are sleeping. Just observe a pet, whether yours or a friend's, that you love while it is asleep. If you open yourself to the experience, unconditional loving will well up inside of you.

After sitting in this experience for a few moments, bring to your awareness the idea that Spirit loves you even more unconditionally than you are loving that sleeping pet. Recognize that the level of Unconditional love you are experiencing for that pet you can give to other people, and to yourself. Finally, turn your attention from the pet to yourself and bring your experience of unconditional loving to yourself.

This exercise helps you to tap into the love that is your true nature. It can be easy to confuse your experience of love in this exercise as dependent upon the pet or the baby, but this is not so. The only love you will ever experience is the love that exists inside of you, as who you are. The pet, baby, spouse, etc. just help you to connect to the essence of Love that is within you and makes you more aware of it. You can't give that which you do not have. The good news is that Spirit, which is who and what we are, is unlimited, unconditional love – and so are you.

## The "I Love..." Game

Another fun way to practice loving is what I call, simply, the "I love..." game. In the "I love..." game you look around your environment for something that you love and call it out. "I love these flowers! I love that wedding photograph! I love the music I am listening to!" Try to find as many things in your environment that you love as you can. The more you play this game with yourself, the more your subconscious will be conditioned to look for things you love and you will experience more of them.

I first began playing this game on my commute to work. Of course, paying primary attention to the traffic around me and being safe because "I love being safe!" After a few commutes, I started noticing flowers everywhere that I had never noticed before. They had always been there but I had never seen them because I was not conditioned to find things I love in my environment.

Once you get really good, you can play the advanced version of the game. In the advanced version, you not only call out the things in your environment that you love, but also why you love them. "I love these roses! I love how they smell and I love the elegant curve of their petals. I love the richness of their color. I love how full they are. I love the experience of beauty I feel when looking at them. I love that I get to experience Life showing up as these flowers and to commune with Spirit through encountering them."

## How Love Helps Bring Complete Emancipation from All Discord of Every Nature

Practicing love is a vital part of any spiritual practice. Love is what and who you truly are. Discord comes from being un-aligned with the Truth of who you are. Complete emancipation from all discord of every nature can only come when you are aligned with your loving nature. Humanity has had a great deal of practice being off of its loving center. Race consciousness conditioned us from very early on.

It will take your attention, intention, and practice to retrain yourself to stay in your loving nature no matter what happens, but it is possible. It may start with getting to a consciously loving experience once a week for 30-seconds, and if that is the case for you, that is absolutely okay. Those 30-seconds will feel great and help propel you forward.

## Treatment regarding Love

*Recognition:* *There is only one Life, one Presence, and one Power. Known by many names, this One is Love itself. It is Unconditional and gives Itself fully and freely to all. This One is unlimited. It is Unlimited, Unconditional Love.*

*Unification:* *As there is only this One, and as I Am, I must therefore be what this One is. I must be Unconditional, Unlimited Love. In this now moment, I identify myself with and as this inexhaustible Love. Love is all there is. Love is all I am. Love is all I can be.*

*Realization:* *Right where I am, there is love, for I Am love. Surrounding me always, is Love, for God is Love and God is all there is. Every plant, every tree, every cloud, is an expression of this perfect love. No matter where I look I have the opportunity to witness and experience love. And so, I turn my attention toward love. I practice loving. Through my intention, attention, and practice, love flows into my life in greater and richer experiences than ever before and there is no limit to how these experiences of love can manifest.*

*I experience love in and for nature. I experience love for all Life. Turning a blind eye to what anybody has ever done, I recognize that the same love that is in me, is in all people. And for this simple reason — that they exist — I love everybody. Whether or not I choose to outwardly express this love, the experience of this basic, Impersonal level of loving occurs within me and uplifts me. As I experience this level of love, more loving flows into my experience and out into the world and, thus, I generate more loving on the planet.*

*For those whom I choose, I practice Direct love. I allow Impersonal love to be upleveled in my experience and the intricacies of personal connection to be present. This is a deeper, more profound level of loving and as I practice it consciously, my experience of loving becomes deeper and more profound. New subtleties of experience flow into my awareness and add a richness to my experience of love that is not available to me in Impersonal love. The more I practice the better I get at opening myself to loving on the personal level, and the more love flows into my experience and through me into the world. Once again, my practice of loving benefits me and the entire planet.*

*Through my practice and intention, I experience Unconditional Love. I see people for who and what they really are — Unconditional Love expressing as human beings. I know that no matter what they may have done, the Unconditional Love that is their true nature is always their true nature and that everything in the Universe works together for harmony.*

*I direct all of these levels of loving toward myself. I recognize that I am Unconditional Love and so, ignoring anything I may have done, I love myself unconditionally. Spirit thought highly enough of me to incarnate as me and so I must be lovable. As I experience myself, I love ME directly. My personality, my quirks, how I show up in the world provides a unique expression of Life and I allow that uniqueness into my experience of loving myself. Finally, I am Unconditional Love and by loving myself Unconditionally, I truly experience who I Am.*

***Thanksgiving:*** *I am so grateful to experience and express loving in so many ways. I give my thanks that the core of who I am is Love and that I have the opportunity to experience love and express my loving in the world, uplifting myself and the entire planet as I radiate my loving self freely.*

***Release:*** *I recognize that everything in this prayer is the Truth. As Truth, there is nothing for me to do, except to release, to let go, to celebrate the victory that is already complete. And so, knowing that this, or something even better for the Highest Good of all is already accomplished, I release this prayer, filled with my enthusiasm and gratitude, and love, into the Universe, knowing that it absolutely returns to me, fulfilled, and then some! Thank you, God. Thank you, Spirit. Thank you, Self of myself. AND SO IT IS!*

# Chapter Eleven

# Spiritual Practice: Compassion

*V*ery closely related to the spiritual practice of Love is Compassion. In fact, love is a required component of compassion and is at the core of its practice.

There are a lot of different ideas about what compassion is, so let's be sure we are on the same page (pun intended), when it comes to compassion.

Compassion is absolutely not, nor does it have anything to do with, sympathy or pity. There is no "feeling sorry for somebody" in compassion. Spiritually speaking, if there is a belief or feeling that something is "wrong" with a situation, then the experience is not one of compassion.

From the spiritual perspective, everything, no matter what it might look like or feel like, is part of the perfect harmony of the Universe, even if we can't possibly fathom how. No matter what the circumstance we, or somebody else, might be going through, the circumstance has contained within it the possibility for growth.

Unfortunately, dictionary definitions of compassion are inadequate from the perspective of spirituality. The closest I have found comes from TheFreeDictonary.com, which defines compassion as "Deep awareness of the suffering of another coupled with the wish to relieve it." This is close, but still inaccurate. In compassion, there is no wish to relieve the suffering of another, because there is the recognition that the suffering is part of what that soul came into this lifetime to learn about. Compassion, rather than a desire to relieve suffering, is the ability to be with somebody while they suffer.

Compassion is really a very sacred thing. The most beneficial thing for somebody going through an experience of suffering is to have somebody with them that can hold a loving space. If I show up doing everything I can to relieve somebody's suffering, it implies that their suffering is wrong, and that the person who is suffering, is "bad" for doing something "wrong."

This isn't to suggest in the slightest that being in the practice of compassion means you desire somebody to suffer. Rather it is a recognition that the only way out of suffering (or any emotional experience) is through that same suffering. If I take away an experience of suffering before it is complete, I am condemning that person to repeat their experience of suffering. Suffering is a rather intense word, so let's use a different example. Let's use math instead, and try to ignore that for many people, math equals suffering.

Imagine a student, Bill, is trying to learn trigonometry. Bill spends weeks and months studying and trying to figure it out. Before he does, however, I come in, take away the textbook and complete all the class assignments for him. Because of this, Bill doesn't learn trigonometry, but because the class was passed, he moves on to physics.

Physics assumes that Bill understands trigonometry and assigns work that requires Bill to know how trigonometry works. Bill does not know how trigonometry works and must go back and learn what he was supposed to learn previously before he can complete the physics assignment in front of him.

It works the same with suffering. A person going through an experience of suffering has the opportunity to learn something very valuable. If I take away their suffering before they have gone through it and learned what the suffering was trying to teach them, then another situation will come about, triggering that same suffering. Instead if you are able to be with a person in their suffering, knowing that despite their experience, they are whole, complete and perfect, you can be the lighthouse that guides the ship safely to shore. The lighthouse doesn't tractor-beam the boat into the harbor; the captain of the boat still has to make the journey him or herself.

That really is what compassion is. Compassion is the light in the darkness of suffering. Rather than holding somebody who is distraught and sobbing and saying, "Shh-hh. Don't cry. No, no. Don't cry. Shhhhh," compassion holds that person and says, "It's okay. What you are feeling is okay. Go ahead and feel it. Let it out. Let it all out. It's okay to cry. I love you." Compassion sits right in the midst of suffering, but does not enter into an experience of suffering. The lighthouse sits right in the midst of darkness, but does not go dark.

Being with suffering in a compassionate way also requires that we not buy into the suffering. When I am being compassionate, I recognize that whomever I am with that is suffering has a growth opportunity before them as they go through their suffering, but I also understand that suffering is not required.

All suffering comes from a misunderstanding of reality. Primarily this misunderstanding is that pain or sadness or upset equals suffering, and this is not so. We can be in an experience of sadness but not be suffering. The suffering comes from resisting the sadness. It comes from the desire to shut out the sadness and not allow it to run its course.

Pain can be pain without suffering. Making the experience of pain wrong takes it from a simple experience of pain and adds a component of suffering to the mix. Pain sucks. Pain hurts. Pain is not something any sane person wants as part of their experience. And, pain can be all of those things without our resisting it and making it wrong.

## Duality

The physical world is a world of duality. We have hot and cold, light and dark, high and low. This contrast is absolutely necessary in the human experience. It is this contrast that helps us to learn and grow. It's this contrast that guides us to greater understanding of ourselves. Contrast is required. Making that contrast wrong instead of using that contrast to learn and grow is what causes suffering.

There is a trap here. It is far too easy, since suffering is optional, to make suffering wrong as well, which will just create more suffering. When we are practicing compassion with others, while recognizing that suffering is optional, we must also make sure to not make their suffering wrong. We must allow them the dignity of their own experience.

## The Dignity of the Experience

This can be a difficult concept to grasp but it is one that is vital to the practice of compassion. There is dignity in every experience, whether we can easily see it or not. Nobody is given more than they can handle in the process of their own spiritual growth and unfoldment. If anybody were given more than they could handle, spiritually speaking, it would be a set-up for failure and that doesn't fit with a God that is Love. The dignity inherent in any and every experience is that through that experience, the individual has the opportunity for growth.

This certainly doesn't mean that you should support the addict in their addiction because of some misplaced idea that there is dignity in addiction. The dignity lies not in the addiction but in the individual's experience of their addiction and their pathway out of it. Many addicts find that, once they are through their addiction, their addiction was actually a blessing, just as many patients with serious illnesses who heal are grateful for the experience of their disease.

Going along with the idea of allowing people the dignity of their own experience is the understanding that everybody does the best they can in the moment. Nobody ever thinks, "Well, choice A is the evil choice and choice B is the good choice so.... choice A!" People do the very best they can with the information and experiences they have at the time. Period.

Think about it. If you really, really knew a certain choice would bring a world of hurt, and were really clear about that, would you make the choice? Of course not! If somebody knows better, they will do better. Thinking, "they should know better!" doesn't matter because even if they "should" know better, they clearly don't, and dwelling on "should" only makes things worse. Everybody does the very best they believe they can based on what they have learned and experienced up to that point, including you.

I had a very powerful example of this in my first semester of college. The class was divided up into three groups. Each group had the same goal in this experiment and each group was bound by the same set of rules. Everybody knew what those rules were. Everything about the game was clear and understood by all. One of the rules was that in order to leave your group's area of the classroom, permission had to be granted by the instructor.

However, the instructor did not grant permission. One group was told, once the game began, that they had permission all the time and didn't need to ask. Another group was given permission most of the time when a member of that group asked for it. The third group, my group, was almost always denied permission. The purpose of this exercise was to give us a different perspective on how people behave when they feel oppressed.

The difference in permission granting was not something the students knew was going to happen. It took me about two minutes to recognize what was going on and about 30 seconds more to decide that the game was unfair and I was not going to follow the rules. I knew there were consequences for breaking the rules, but the rules were already broken from my perspective so I didn't care. I began seeing how much I could get away with. How many rules could I break before I got caught? I didn't care if I got caught because I believed that the only way I could even come close to keeping up with the other groups was to break the rules.

Generally speaking, I follow the rules. I follow the rules not because I don't want to receive the punishment from breaking the rules, but because that is what is in alignment for me. In this experience, it took less than three minutes for me to completely change and break every rule I could, regardless of the consequences.

Yes, I knew what the rules were and yes, I knew I was supposed to follow them. But from my experience, from what I believed to be true, the rules were there to keep me stuck while advancing other people and, what did it matter if I got in trouble for breaking the rules? I wasn't going to win the game anyway.

This was a very eye-opening experience for me, for while I knew the rules I didn't "know better" enough to follow them. This certainly doesn't absolve me of responsibility in my choices. I chose to break the rules. However, I came to see how easy it was for me to know what "I should do" and not do it. I did the best I believed I could in that circumstance, even though I was breaking the rules. We all do the best we believe that we can, all the time.

## Compassion for Yourself

This story brings up a very important piece with the practice of compassion. Up until now, the discussion has been all about being compassionate with others. Compassion with others is very important, but just as important (if not more so) is compassion with yourself. Being compassionate toward somebody else is far easier than being compassionate with yourself and so practicing with other people can be very helpful. Ultimately the goal is compassion toward yourself. I am my own worst critic. We all are. People tend to hold themselves to a much higher standard than they hold other people, often times to a standard that is unreasonable.

Nobody would expect somebody who has never held a golf club before to drive 250 yards on their first swing. Hitting the ball at all is an accomplishment, let alone hitting it straight or far. Yet, when you pick up that club and miss a few swings are you more likely to become embarrassed and criticize yourself, or to continue swinging free from a personal berating?

Early on in my reconnection with my spiritual practice, in a spiritual counseling session, the person I was counseling with called me out on just such a lack of compassion for myself. "That is not being very nice to Ben," he said, "and I won't stand for anybody, even you, being that mean to Ben." It was quite an eye-opener and helped me to realize the importance of compassion toward myself. Since then, I have used that same line when I catch myself not being compassionate toward myself. It is a great reminder for me.

## Why Have Self-Compassion

While there are plenty of touchy-feely reasons why compassion toward yourself is essential, there is a quite simple and profound practical reason as well: Compassion compels growth, while criticism sustains suffering. Let's go back to the golf example.

Imagine you have just signed up for golf lessons. It's your first time on the driving range with the instructor. You set up, take a swing, and totally miss the ball! The instructor looks at you with disdain and says, "You didn't even hit the ball. What is wrong with you?" How likely are you to hit the ball on your second try? Not very. Are you more likely to complete your lesson, or quit golf all together before the hour is up?

Instead, imagine that after swinging and missing the instructor says, "Hey, you got closer to hitting the ball on your first swing than a lot of people do. Seriously. You might think that sucked, but you actually did well for your first swing. Give it another try." Clearly, hearing this from an instructor instead is far more likely to produce growth in your hitting the ball and you would be far more likely to enjoy the lesson and continue with your golf practice.

Now, for the real kicker... Imagine that instead of an instructor saying these things to you, it is you saying these things to yourself. In one way or another, at one time or another, we have all said similar things to ourselves. We have all been compassionate with ourselves and compelled ourselves to grow, and we have all been harshly critical and sustained our own suffering.

## Compassion and the Interconnection of Life

Through the practice of compassion, we are able to build our awareness of, and experience the interconnection between all life. As our awareness of our connection to everybody else grows, compassion becomes more natural and easy. All life is connected. There is only one life and that is the life of Spirit. We are all individual expressions of Spirit and we all live Spirit's life as us. One wave in the ocean is connected by the ocean to each and every other wave. The practice of compassion requires the recognition that you are connected to my experience and I am connected to yours.

John Bradford was a minister in England in the early 1500's. He was imprisoned in the Tower of London for alleged crimes against Mary Tudor for his Protestant faith. While in the Tower, he would witness fellow prisoners being led to their execution and say to himself, "There but for the grace of God, goes John Bradford." From this, the phrase, "there but for the grace of God, go I" originated and it is a wonderful phrase to remind us of the interconnection of all life and urge us toward compassion.

A simplified way of saying "there but for the grace of God, go I" is to say "that could be me." That could be me and the only reason it isn't me is because of the way grace has shown up in my life. I was born in the United States, not in a war-torn, poverty-stricken third-world country where most people live on less than two dollars a day and children die of starvation in very high numbers. Why? Why was I born in one place and not another? What did I do to get born here and not there? The answer, of course, is nothing. I didn't do anything to be born here instead of there. There but for the grace of God, go I.

Starvation and poverty could just as easily have been my experience as being born just outside of what is considered poverty in the United States. While poverty and starvation are not my direct experience, I am connected to that experience in two ways.

First, spiritually speaking, there is only one Life, which is God or Spirit and all of us are individual expressions of that one life, so even though I am not in the experience of starvation, somebody living on the same life energy as I am, is experiencing starvation. Secondly, I am part of the human race and as such, am connected to all of the experiences of humanity.

Carl Jung, founder of analytical psychology, describes this interconnection of all life as the collective unconscious. This collective unconscious is a repository of everything ever experienced by any individual. Everybody's experience goes into the collective unconscious and so everybody is connected to the experiences of everybody else.

Through the collective unconscious we have access to the entirety of human experience. Since we are all connected to the collective unconscious it is part of who we are and so too is every experience contained within it. From this perspective, we have all been murdered and murderers. We have all been male and female, every race, religion, and creed.

Recognizing this, it becomes much easier for me to bring compassion to my interactions with other people. Their experience will go into the collective unconscious and at that level, become my experience too.

## Compassion Relieves Upset

Compassion is also a brilliant reliever of upset, whether that upset is directed toward others or toward yourself. In order to be in the practice of compassion, you must bring love into the equation. Love and upset cannot sustainably coexist. In the presence of love, upset diminishes.

Ultimately, if you are able to bring complete unconditional love into an experience of upset, the upset will vanish as quickly as the darkness does when you turn on a light. Short of that grand ideal, any amount of love brought to an experience of upset will start to transmute the upset. The speed and degree to which it does depends on the degree of the loving we bring to the upset.

A very unexpected yet powerful experience of this happened for me right around Christmas of 2013. A certain young pop star announced that he would be retiring from music. I must admit, I used to have a good deal of animosity toward him. I didn't like the image he was projecting to his fan base, or what I perceived his attitude to be. I was NOT a fan. After announcing his pending retirement, Facebook posts became filled with comments like, "My Christmas wish came true!"

There was so much venom in these comments that my compassionate heart was engaged powerfully, and seemingly of its own accord. I began to "put myself in his shoes." What would it feel like if, on one hand I was so successful and, on the other, had so much hate directed toward me?

I can see how difficult that experience could be from the perspective of an adult (me) with a decade of solid spiritual practice under my belt. How difficult must that be for a youth who, instead of hearing whispers from teachers urging spiritual exploration, hears shouts of fans, venom from non-fans, and greed from producers and an industry that would sooner squeeze every possible penny rather than support the development of consciousness?

This questioning put me in an experience of impersonal love as I disregarded this performer's words and actions that I thought were "wrong." With this foundation of love in place and knowing that "there but for the grace of God, goes Ben Jamison," I fell into an experience of compassion for this fellow soul, learning about himself through what could easily be viewed as far more difficult circumstances than my own, despite his wealth. This compassion dissolved my upset about him and since that experience, no upset has returned.

Bringing compassion into your experience, with and toward yourself, is essential to an effective spiritual practice and to your growth. Remember, compassion means to be with suffering. When we are engaging in compassion for others, this is a bit more straight forward, but with yourself it can get a little murky. How, when I am in the experience of suffering, do I be consciously present to the experience of suffering, while not buying into suffering (as true compassion requires) and not make the suffering wrong? It can twist the mind in knots!

Compassion toward yourself is done through awareness and intention. First, you must become aware that you are in an experience that calls for compassion – and no experience is too small or trivial for compassion. Once you are aware that you are suffering to any degree, you can make the experience okay and bring a blanket of loving to it.

As an example of this, one of the courses I took in my Master's degree in Spiritual Psychology required me to spend time observing people in various age groups with the intention of bringing forward any memories from that age stage in my life that could use some healing. It came time for the observation of the age group 12-20 and I found myself in a coffee shop with my lovely wife (who also holds a Master's in Spiritual Psychology) observing an employee in his late teens.

As memories from that stage in my life came forward, I began to get very uncomfortable. This was a very awkward age in my life, as it is for many people. The longer the observation went on, the more the memories of that awkwardness and feeling out of place came into my experience.

The course work required the observation last at least 30 minutes and I quickly noticed that I was checking the time frequently, hoping the half hour was up so that I could stop the observation and with it, those uncomfortable feelings (aka: suffering) that I was experiencing. My breathing became labored and heavy, with lots of sighing.

My wife, keenly aware of what was going on, said, "Just be with it, Honey." Just be with it. I was so resistant to the feeling I was experiencing that I was creating suffering in the midst of the experience. Her loving reminder to be compassionate toward myself brought my awareness to the suffering I was experiencing.

With the light of that awareness, I was able to make those awkward feelings be okay. Doing so did not remove the awkward feelings, in fact it increased them, but the suffering component was gone. Without energy being spent in suffering, I was able to bring forward more of the memories and feelings from that time in my life for healing than I would have been able to, had I not brought compassion to myself.

## Compassion Supports Growth

This story is also a perfect example of how compassion helps to support us and others as we grow. The exercise of the observation was intended to bring forward feelings and memories that needed to be healed. The suffering that I was engaged in through my resistance to feeling the feelings that were coming forward was taking up "bandwidth" and holding off my experience of what would result in personal healing and growth. Bringing compassion to the suffering, and making my feelings okay, opened up more space for me to feel and remember – all in service to my growth.

Compassion also supports growth for ourselves and those we engage with because it doesn't buy into the suffering as a requirement. Remember that suffering is caused by resistance and wrong-making. If a loved one of my dear friend passes away, there is likely to be the experience of sadness and loss for my friend. It goes with the territory. That experience of sadness and loss does not require suffering, yet the resistance to "what is" often causes suffering in the experience.

If I am to be with my dear friend, while holding onto suffering as being required of the experience of the passing of a loved one, it's possible that I will create a discordant atmosphere that could prolong the suffering. If I am uncomfortable with my dear friend's full expression of their grief, they will be less likely to allow their grief full expression. When we keep such feelings inside, instead of letting them come up and out, they grow and fester within us.

If, on the other hand, I encourage my dear friend to feel all of the pain and loss they are feeling, and remind them that feeling those feelings is not wrong, but rather is perfectly okay, they will be able to more completely express what is present for them.

Remember, the way out of any experience is through the full expression of the experience. As I provide, through my compassionate heart, the safe and loving space for my dear friend to really, *really* have the fullness of their experience, they will come through it quicker and more completely. Plus, by encouraging my dear friend to remember that their experience is okay, and thus keeping the suffering out of their "emotional bandwidth" they will have more room to feel what they need to feel, just as I did during my observation of the young man in the coffee shop.

While the death of a loved one is a pretty extreme example, this holds true in any situation where compassion is called for.

The other way that compassion helps in supporting growth is that compassion helps us to see through the story that is creating the suffering. There is a fine line between experiencing what is present and to be worked through, and spinning around in the same story over and over again (possibly using different words and context) and not making any forward progress. The keys to telling the difference are in the loving aspect of compassion, and awareness. Being aware that there is a tendency for us, that is, all of us human beings, to get stuck in our story is the first step. Once we are aware of this tendency is it much easier to notice it. Congratulations, you are now aware!

The stories we tell ourselves about the events that take place in our lives are not what actually took place. They are our recollections of what took place, colored by our consciousness at the time. Often times, when related to the experience of suffering, the stories we tell ourselves and others about the situation contain the judgments and resistance that is perpetuating our experience of suffering. The sooner we move into acceptance that what happened, happened, and stop making it wrong, the sooner we can heal and grow. Compassion helps to bring us to that acceptance.

Earlier on, I told how at one point in my life, I believed that I was unlovable. If I had continued to replay the story that I had been telling myself, which led me to the belief that I was unlovable, I would still believe it. Luckily, somebody with a compassionate heart helped me to stop telling the same story.

When we are being with somebody, or ourselves, in a compassionate way, loving is at the core of what we are doing. That loving essence allows us to get some space between our awareness and the experience. Remember, we are not making the experience wrong in any way but, by getting some space, we can more easily recognize an old story dressed up all fancy. By getting the space and stopping the unconscious storytelling, we can begin to tell ourselves a new story, one that we actually want to experience.

## Compassion as a Way of Being

Compassion, while being a spiritual practice, is also a way of being that, through your practice, you cultivate within yourself. In order to do so, it is vital to come from a different perspective than the world generally holds. Remember, the spiritual viewpoint is that everything is part of a greater harmony and that suffering in an individual's experience, while not required, is helping that individual to learn and grow. This perspective is so important because it is what will keep you from dropping into wanting to remove the suffering for the individual, rather than supporting them as they move through their suffering.

Another aspect of this harmony is that there is never a situation put before anybody that they are not able to work through. If there were, it would not be harmonious. No matter what may be happening in somebody's experience, they are perfectly capable of going through the experience in such a way as to learn and grow from it.

If we are going to be in a compassionate space with somebody we must recognize that they are capable of handling what is in front of them to handle. This, by the way, includes you. You must recognize that you are capable (far more than capable, in fact) of handling whatever is in front of you to handle.

In the beginning, this will take conscious effort. I still have to remind myself to bring my compassionate heart into play from time to time. Over time and with practice, being compassionate will happen more easily and naturally.

I have to remind myself much less frequently than I used to. Eventually, compassion will not be just a tool you use, but rather an integrated aspect of who you are.

## How Compassion Helps Bring Complete Emancipation from All Discord of Every Nature

Compassion is vital to the elimination of discord. Basically, being compassionate means being in an experience where suffering (or discord) is, not making it wrong, and surrounding the whole thing in a blanket of love. Doing so tends to lessen, or ideally, eliminate the suffering from the experience.

Remember, compassion will not remove sadness, or physical pain, or frustration. It will take the suffering from those and other such experiences. Sadness is not wrong. Suffering is added to sadness when we decide that it is. As we become more adept at being compassionate with ourselves, our experiences of suffering and discord will diminish.

## Treatment regarding Compassion

*Recognition: There is only one Life. This Life is perfect. This Life is the perfect Life of God. God is Love, unconditioned. God is Compassion, ever present.*

*Unification: As there is only one Life, the Life that is God, it must also be the Life that I live. As such, all that God is is available to me, in me, as me. The Unconditional Love that is God is centered in my being. The Compassion that is God is centered in my being.*

*Realization: Compassion flows from every bit of my being. Compassion is natural to me. As I focus my attention on compassion and bringing compassion to myself and those around me, my experience of compassion in my life expands. I am reminded through my practice of compassion that all life is connected and so I love and am compassionate toward all.*

*The loving center of my compassion sees through my "story" and clears away my experience of suffering. The more compassionate I am with myself, the more powerfully and clearly I work through the experiences of sadness and find more richness in every taste of joy.*

*As I put my attention on the practice of compassion it becomes quickly and gracefully integrated into how I show up in the world. Compassion is my way of being, naturally expressing whenever and wherever it can be of benefit.*

*Thanksgiving: I am so grateful for my compassionate heart. I am overjoyed that compassion is part of who I am and naturally fills my life. I am blessed and honored to be compassionate with others and so grateful for the service I am able to provide for others, and myself, as we all learn and grow in our spiritual awakening.*

*Release: I release this prayer into the law of creation, knowing that as it has been spoken in unification with the Divine Life of all Life, it is already done. I claim it good and very good. This, or something even better for the Highest Good of all concerned already is. Thank you God. And So It IS!!!*

# Chapter Twelve

## Spiritual Practice: Meditation

*M*editation is one of the most essential components of many spiritual practice. Through meditation you are able to powerfully experience your connection with Spirit. Meditation helps to keep you centered regardless of what is happening around you. It energizes you and builds your intuitive capacity. Meditation reminds you of who you truly are as an individual expression of Spirit.

Many scientific studies, published in respected scientific journals, highlight the vast array of health benefits meditation provides. Meditation lowers blood pressure, improves social interactions, and aids in learning. The power of a meditative practice to beneficially impact your life cannot be overstated.

Merriam-Webster defines the verb meditate as "to engage in mental exercise (such as concentration on one's breathing or repetition of a mantra) for the purpose of reaching a heightened level of spiritual awareness." To a certain degree, this definition is correct. Heightened levels of spiritual awareness are certainly a result of meditation; however, I would not define them as the purpose.

The purpose of meditation is to know yourself more deeply and accurately. Through this greater connection to an awareness of your true nature, all the other benefits of meditation spring. Heightened spiritual awareness, lower blood pressure, and feeling more calm and centered are all wonderful side effects of a meditative practice, but they are not the point or the purpose.

## What Is Meditation?

It is difficult to describe what meditation is because meditation is experienced differently by everybody and is, to a certain degree, beyond description. Generally speaking, however, meditation is a deep silence and stillness with an inner, single-pointed focus. In meditation there is a disassociation with the external, physical world. The meditator becomes inwardly focused and the outside world tends to melt away or become very diffused. Meditation is extremely relaxing and rejuvenating. A short time spent in meditation can refresh like nothing else.

In meditation, as with all spiritual practices, there is not really a right way or wrong way to meditate. The "wrong way" to meditate is a way that doesn't work for you. The "right way" is the way that does. There are many, many techniques of meditation that you can explore. I have explored several meditation techniques, and found benefit from all of them. (At the end of the book is a resource list you might find helpful.) There are meditation practices that occur while sitting and there are others that are done while walking. I know a lovely woman who finds meditation in doing laundry.

No matter what meditation technique you use, there are a few things to keep in mind when establishing a meditation practice.

**The technique is not the meditation.** The meditation technique, whether it be Transcendental Meditation®, contemplative meditation, mindfulness, or any other, is not meditation. It is what takes you to the meditation. My primary meditation technique has recently shifted from Transcendental Meditation or TM to mantra meditation. As these two techniques have provided the bulk of my meditative experiences, all of the examples in this book will be discussed from the perspective and experiences I have had with mantra meditation and TM. While there are differences in techniques, the broad strokes of all meditative practices are generally universal.

In mantra meditation, a name of God (Ram, Spirit, I Am, Love, etc.) is silently repeated over and over and over again. As the mind becomes more and more focused on the mantra from the repetitions, the outside world falls away and eventually the mantra itself falls away. Once the mantra falls away you are in meditation. The repetition of the mantra is not the meditation but the pathway to the meditation. The same holds true for any meditation technique. The technique that you are doing is not meditation, for meditation is being, not doing.

**Meditation is active, not passive.** More accurately put, meditation is both active and passive at the same time. Sitting relaxed and passive is a wonderful experience for sure. It is refreshing and does help to re-center and energize. The mind may wander and drift. It goes where it may and we follow it wherever it goes. In meditation, however, there is a very active intention happening.

Speaking from my experience with mantra meditation, when I meditate I am very active in my focus on the mantra. When my mind wanders, I guide it back (gently) into focus. There is strong intention present in the practice. However, there is no attachment. I am very focused on the mantra, but am not attached to it. I allow it to go away. When the mantra goes away, the focus does not.

This is one of the paradoxes around meditation and something that is far more difficult to describe than it is to experience. In meditation the body and the mind become still. This stillness looks, and is, very passive. It looks like nothing is happening, and in one sense nothing *is* happening. On the other hand, to the extent that the meditation brings you into alignment with Spirit, *everything* is happening. There is incredible focus in meditation, yet the goal is non-attachment. Keeping the mind from wandering off and daydreaming is a very active practice. Not getting upset when the mind wanders and gently bringing it back into focus requires un-attachment and passivity.

**Nothing in meditation is done fast or hard.** Everything is soft, gentle and slow. When the focus wanders off, slamming it back into place will be very jarring and tend to knock you back into awareness of the physical.

Slowly, gently, and lovingly directing the mind back into focus deepens the meditation. In the practice of mantra meditation, if the mantra is repeated 100 times in one minute, there is no way the meditator will ever "drop in" to the meditation. Even the thought of trying to mantra 100 times in one minute stresses me out! Instead the mantra is repeated calmly and slowly. It is consistent but not fast. It flows, just flows.

**You may have no idea you are actually meditating.** While you very well could be completely aware that you are in the meditation while you are in the midst, it is also possible that you will not realize it until after the meditation. I once sat down to meditate with a timer set for 20 minutes. I closed my eyes and began to mantra. In what I would have sworn was no more than two minutes later, the timer went off. That seemingly 18-minute time gap was meditation. I had no idea I was in it while I was in it, but once I came out of it, I was very much aware of the experience.

When these experiences of time compression in meditation first started happening in my practice, I was ecstatic!  After a while, I began to find frustration with those experiences.  I wanted to be aware of being in meditation while being in meditation. Yeah, it was great to have the awareness afterward, but I wanted more. What I was getting wasn't good enough...

Then it stopped happening.  I didn't begin having experiences of being aware of the meditation while in the meditation.  I stopped "dropping in" to the mediation all together.  It took me about a year of diligent practice to start "dropping in" again.

The moral of this story is two-fold.  First, meditation for you will be what is right for you.  Don't judge your experience.  It is what it is for a reason and judging it will **not** make it better.

Secondly, it can take a long time of practicing before really rich experiences are present.  Don't let this dissuade you.  Whether or not a 20-minute session seems like 20 minutes, 2 minutes, or 2 hours does not matter.  Any and every second spent in the practice of meditation is invaluable.

## Establishing Your Meditation Practice: Excuses and Answers

Establishing a meditation practice is not easy.  It is very simple, but not at all easy.  What is easy is finding excuses to not establish a meditation practice.  "I don't have time," is a common and rather effective excuse, at least at the beginning.  We are all busy.  It seems there are multiple things competing for your attention most of the time and now here I am throwing meditation at you as another one.  "You want me to take time out of my busy schedule to sit still?" Yup. And whether you realize it or not yet, you want you to take that time too.

Not all time spent is equal. Time spent being bored on social media in the avoidance of doing things you don't want to do has a certain type of "return on investment." Time spent in meditation provides the greatest return on investment you can get.

I am committed to meditation for a minimum of 10 minutes each day. Most often, I do two 20-minute sessions daily, but on rare occasion I do my minimum. And I notice a difference. On the days when I meditate for a total of 40 minutes I have more energy and have it more consistently. My mood is better on those days and I am far more productive. I get more accomplished and am more joyful in the accomplishing when I spend more time in meditation.

It has been quite a long time since I have missed a day of meditation all together. If I were to forget to meditate in the morning, I would find that by the afternoon I would be grumpy and little things that normally wouldn't bother me would get under my skin. When I notice such experiences, I stop whatever I am doing and meditate. Afterward, I feel more like myself again.

The excuse of "not enough time" is completely false. It may seem very real. Believe me, I know. I didn't have a regular mediation practice once. I made the "not enough time" excuse over and over again. These days, the busier and more stressful my day looks, the more important meditation becomes.

"I would meditate, but I just can't sit still for that long." Once again, at first this seems like a totally valid excuse. Sitting still for longs periods of time can be difficult. We aren't used to it. Society programs us to be on the go all the time.

However, everybody remains still for many hours while sleeping. We have all had the experience of being totally engrossed in a movie and not moving a muscle for the two plus hours of the film. So, "I can't sit still for that long" is a false statement. We all can, and we all do.

Another reason why this excuse is inaccurate is that when establishing a meditation practice, you don't start at twenty minutes. You start at two, or even one. The world record for the bench press is 722 pounds. The dude who did that (Eric Spoto) didn't start out anywhere close to putting 722 pounds on a bar. The experiences I am sharing about meditation have taken several years of practice to happen, and I am nowhere close to being a master meditator.

When I started learning to meditate I wouldn't even come close to dropping in. As always, start right where you are and make where you are okay, because it is okay. Over time, you will be able to sit for longer periods of time. Over time, you will be able to focus for longer. Over time, you will establish a wonderfully supportive meditation practice.

"My life is just fine. I don't need to worry about meditation. If I needed it I would work on it, but I don't." Your life may well be just fine. However, given that you are reading this book, it is safe to assume that you want more out of life than you are currently getting. Meditation is one of the best ways to improve the quality of your life. As your meditation practice deepens, so too does your connection to Spirit. The more connected you feel to Source, the more love, joy, gratitude, excitement, energy, etc. you will experience.

Have you ever had the experience of thinking that you weren't very hungry, only to find yourself ravenous after just a few bites of food? Meditation is kind of like that. It may seem that you don't need to meditate, if you don't already have a practice, but once you get that first taste of a good meditation, you are likely to realize how hungry for it you truly are. Meditation gives you a greater experience of yourself. The more you meditate, the more you come to realize your true nature.

There are limitless excuses to avoid establishing a meditation practice. I cannot possibly go into them all here, but there is one more that must be addressed before moving on: Meditation is a life-long practice. Some people take to it like a fish to water and others struggle for years before having consistently fulfilling meditations. If the results you are seeking are not coming fast enough, it can be very easy to quit. However, whether or not progress is noticeable, rest assured that it is happening.

You don't have to be a meditation master to gain great benefit from a meditation practice. Like I said earlier, I am far from a master meditator, yet the results of my meditation practice in my life are extraordinary.

There is more good news. No matter how accomplished you become at meditation, there will always be more to grow into. Somebody who has meditated every day for 50 years will have even more profound meditative experiences after 51 years of practice.

## Establishing Your Meditation Practice: Two Keys for Success

There are two keys to establishing a meditation practice that will really help to make sure you succeed in establishing a deep, beneficial practice. The first of these keys is to start small and build up over time. There is no amount of time that is too short to begin with. If one minute seems like a good starting point, start there. If one minute seems like too big of a stretch, go for 45 seconds. Don't rush your build-up either; if you need to stay at one minute, daily, for a month, then do so. Remember, this is a life-long practice. Once your starting time feels comfortable, you can increase by one minute, or several.

Another aspect of starting small and building up to greater and greater amounts of time is to use a timer as part of your meditation practice. If you set a timer, you can forget about how long it has been and just let the timer bring you out of your meditation when your practice time has elapsed. At first, your brain will likely question how long you have been practicing less than a minute after you begin. If a timer is running, it is far easier to let those thoughts go.

Also, forget about any grand ideas of meditation for an hour at a time. You may well work up to that, you may not. I know people who have been meditating for over 20 years who do about 20 minutes at a time. As of the writing of this book, I do two sessions of 20 minutes of meditation. I would like to do more, and when the time is right I will. I don't know when that will be, but when it is time to increase my time I'll know it. You will know too.

The second of these two keys is consistency and commitment. Commitment has incredible power.

> "I believe life is constantly testing us for our level of commitment, and life's greatest rewards are reserved for those who demonstrate a never-ending commitment to act until they achieve. This level of resolve can move mountains, but it must be constant and consistent. As simplistic as this may sound, it is still the common denominator separating those who live their dreams from those who live in regret."
>
> ~Anthony Robbins

When I was taught mantra meditation, I actually signed a written commitment with my teacher. I committed to meditating for at least ten minutes every day. That signed commitment has been a great support in encouraging me to continue with my practice.

Consistency is also of vital importance. Just like any new skill, the more consistently you practice the quicker your skill will advance. For a while in my practice, I was committed to meditating Monday through Friday, but not on the weekends. Once I committed to the consistency of daily meditation, my practice deepened quickly. Daily consistency helps establish meditation as a habit. It becomes built into the morning routine, for example, so remembering to practice isn't an issue.

## Beginning Meditation Exercise

The following is a very simple practice to begin your experimentation with meditation. It will help give you an idea of how beneficial meditation can be and also start to get you used to having a meditation practice. I highly encourage you to explore a variety of meditation techniques to find what works for you, or to pull your own together from various aspects of various techniques. This little exercise combines some aspects of Mindfulness and Mantra meditation techniques. The following technique is very simple, so I suggest reading through the process once and then trying it. It will only take a few minutes.

First, find a comfortable place to sit where you will not be disturbed. Sit in whatever way is comfortable for you. Different techniques suggest different body positions, but for this exercise, being upright and comfortable are the only requirements.

Notice your body. How do you feel in this moment? Don't try to change anything and don't make how you are feeling right or wrong, just notice it.

Now, set a timer for two minutes (or just one if two seems like too much) and close your eyes. Let go of everything. Don't "try" to "do" anything. Focus on your breath, but don't try to control your breath. Let your breath come and go all on its own. As your body breathes in, think "I am breathing in." Allow this sentence to span the entire length of your inhale. As your body exhales, think "I am breathing out." Again, have the thought last as long as your exhale. In the pauses between the inhale and exhale, simply wait silently for the next breath cycle to begin. If your thoughts wander, gently bring your focus back to your breath and "I am breathing in....I am breathing out." Continue this process until the timer goes off.

Notice your body again. How do you feel now? What differences do you notice? Are you more relaxed, more peaceful? How is your breathing different? Is your mind-chatter quieter? Just notice.

∽

If two minutes was easy, try five. When you notice yourself feeling stressed, take one minute to do this exercise and see what results. You could easily expand this exercise and have it become your meditation practice while you explore other techniques, or permanently if it works well. If you shift your focus to the Third Eye (the slight divot in your forehead just above the space between the eyebrows), drop the "breathing in, breathing out" part so all you have left is "I Am" (a name of God) and silently repeat "I Am" over and over, you have a mantra meditation.

## How Meditation Helps Bring Complete Emancipation from all Discord of Every Nature

Meditation helps connect you to Spirit. In truth, you are always connected to Spirit, but meditation helps you to attune to that ever-present connection. There is no discord in Spirit. The more conscious you become of your connection to Spirit, the easier you're able to draw upon that inexhaustible source of peace, calmness, grace, love, and joy. Pulling these energies into your body and experiences transmutes discord.

I hope that in the brief meditation exercise you felt a difference in your body and your experience. It may have been subtle, but odds are good that after those few minutes you felt more centered and at peace. Experiencing a peaceful center is a great way of describing complete emancipation from all discord of every nature.

A somewhat less "woo-woo" way that meditation helps to get us out of discordant experiences is by quieting our thinking mind. A commonly held belief is that the brain has anywhere from 20,000 to 70,000 thoughts a day. In my research I couldn't find an actual scientific study confirming that estimation, but regardless of if it's 70,000, 50,000, or 10,000 thoughts every day, that's a whole lot of thinking.

All that thinking can be overwhelming, especially considering that if we are honest, a lot of those thoughts are negative and stressful. Getting a break from all that thinking, especially the negative thinking, clearly reduces discord. Fewer thoughts equal less discordant thoughts. Fewer discordant thoughts equal fewer discordant experiences. Remember, it is your consciousness that creates your experience and consciousness is built, in part, by what you think.

## Treatment regarding Meditation

*Recognition:  There is only one Life, one Presence, and one Power.  This Life is perfect, complete, and whole in every way, shape and form. It is always centered for It is all there is, and can therefore never be disconnected from anything.  It is always peaceful for everything is always well in Spirit.*

*Unification: I Am that one Life.  It is the only Life there is so it must be the Life that I live and everything that is true of that Life must be true of me.  This Life, centered everywhere, is centered in me.  The peace of this Life is present right where I am, in me and as me.  That which this Life is, I Am.*

*Realization:  As one with this perfect Life, I am always connected to It.  Through meditation, I attune my awareness to this connection and draw from this limitless source all the peace, power, life, love, joy, creativity, and energy that I need to remain calm, centered, and powerful throughout the day.  My meditation practice fills me with this divine Light and energy.  Beginning with my meditation practice right where it is, I experience phenomenal results.  As I deepen my commitment to and my consistency with my meditation practice it grows easily and gracefully.*

*The perfect technique, teacher, or inspiration that I need to establish and grow my meditation practice shows up at the perfect right timing, for the entire Universe conspires for my highest good in my meditative endeavors. All the energy, alertness, and time that I need to establish and grow my meditation practice is available to me now, through my un-severable connection to Spirit, the one Source of all things.*

*__Thanksgiving:__ I am so grateful for knowing that I am one with Spirit. Gratitude pours forth from me as my meditation practice manifests and grows in perfection.*

*__Release:__ I release. I let go. This prayer is perfect. It has been received by Spirit and answered. The answer, as always, is yes! Knowing that this, or something even better for the Highest Good of all concerned already is, I affirm this truth with Spirit by saying, And So It Is!*

# Chapter Thirteen

## Spiritual Practice:
## Visualization and Manifestation

Visualization is like daydreaming with a purpose. Aside from being exceptionally fun, visualization is also a very effective spiritual practice that does wonders for the manifestation of your desires and the progression of your spiritual practice.

You can visualize an amazing place to live or a car you want to own. You can visualize having the perfect job or a loving relationship. You can visualize yourself as an accomplished meditator or as having established a wonderfully fulfilling spiritual practice and relationship with Spirit. There are very few limits to what visualization can be used for.

The guidelines are the same as for Affirmative Prayer. Does your desire harm no one? Does your desire bring only a benefit for all involved? Would you want your desire for everybody? If the answer to these questions is yes, then visualize away.

Does your desire come at the expense of somebody else? Do you want your desire only for yourself and hope others are excluded from experiencing the same in their life? If so, then using any spiritual practice, including visualization, to attain your desire is unwise.

What you put your energy into comes back to you, through cause and effect. If you energetically visualize harm toward another, it will come back to you. Conversely, if that which you desire is for the Highest Good of all concerned, then your desire comes to you as your Highest Good.

## Forming the Mold

As you visualize something you desire you begin to form the mold for the manifestation of that desire. For anything to happen to you, it must happen through you. You must give shape to your desires in order for them to manifest. Have you ever had the experience of wanting *something* but were not sure what that something was? How successful were you in fulfilling that desire? You can't fulfill a desire if you don't know what would cause that desire to be fulfilled.

Often times, we do know what would fulfill our desire, yet we lack a certain amount of clarity. If you need a vehicle and, when asked what you want, you reply, "You know, a vehicle," you are quite far off from fulfilling that desire. Do you want a car or a truck? Do you want two doors, two and a hatchback, four doors, station wagon, minivan? Visualization helps to provide the clarity you need in order to take action toward manifesting your desires.

## Quicken Manifestation

Visualization also speeds up the process of manifestation and draws your desires toward you. We have all heard the saying "I'll believe it when I see it." Well, guess what?! Scientific studies, dating back to the work of Edmund Jacobson in 1931 (and many since then), tell us that the body can't tell the difference between a real experience and a vividly imagined experience.

Jacobson had people imagine bending their arm and found that the flexor muscles in the arm contracted slightly from the imagined movement. So, if you are a "believe it when I see it" person, visualize! See it in your mind's eye and your body won't know the difference.

The more your body feels that what you desire is already in your experience, through visualization, the more the energy of your body will become a magnet, pulling your desire to you.

The more your body believes that your desire has already arrived, the more your desire will become integrated into your subconscious mind as already being present in your experience.

The subconscious is extremely powerful in creating our experience. There is far too much information being gathered every second for us to consciously handle all of it. Our subconscious edits all of the information we receive, allowing only the most important or relevant information to reach our conscious awareness.

A subconscious that believes a desire is already in place will present information to your conscious mind that is aligned with that belief. You can then act on that information, which is what will ultimately lead to the manifestation of what you're seeking.

## Expand Awareness of What Is Possible

The more we practice visualization the more our awareness expands. When I first began to visualize what my ideal relationship would be like, my best imagining was at a "level 1." The best that I could imagine was, quite frankly, not very good.

However, once I got good at visualizing a level 1 type of relationship, I was able to start pulling in some level 2 ideas.

Before long, I was up to visualizing a level 5 relationship, then a 6. When level 1 is the best you can imagine, level 6 is impossible. But, like with everything, we have to start where we are. Eventually I was able to visualize a 10+ relationship (and ended up manifesting far better than that).

Futurists and science fiction writers are perfect examples of how visualization expands our awareness of what is possible. They imagine how a technology might advance over time and visualize what new uses the advanced technology might have. By building upon these visualizations, their minds open to new possibilities that have never before been.

I heard a radio story recently about the scientists who worked on Voyager I, the first manmade object to leave our solar system. As a boy, one of these scientists loved science fiction. When he received the telegram informing him that he had been selected to work on Voyager I, science fiction became his reality.

The same holds true for us. Some of the things we desire may seem like fantasy, but through visualization you can begin to feel the possibility of your desires. Riding on this feeling, you can visualize deeper and more powerful experiences of that which you desire. Eventually, by building upon those feelings and *taking action*, you can come to the place where the experience is no longer imagined but is your physical world experience.

## Engage the Universe

Visualization also engages the Universe in your manifestation efforts. The Universe understands the language of visualization. It's kind of like trying to place an order with a waiter who speaks a language you don't speak. It is very hard to get that waiter to help you.

However, once you speak the same language it becomes easy. It is a friendly Universe. The entire Universe conspires for your highest good to be fulfilled. It wants to support you in your spiritual practice and in the manifestation of other desires, but the Universe cannot help you unless you give it something to work with.

Our images and experiences in visualization give the Universe what it needs to start moving. The clearer, more powerful and more frequent your visualization, the more engaged the Universe will be.

Does it sound crazy, the idea that the Universe itself will start moving based on your visualizations? If so, simply substitute Spirit or God for Universe. This may still seem farfetched, but once you have a manifestation experience with synchronicities beyond explanation, it will make sense.

Allow me to share just such an experience from my life.

When my wife and I began planning our wedding, we were having a very difficult time. We were trying to somehow create an abundant feeling wedding from a wedding budget that didn't seem like it would support an abundant feeling wedding.

After an evening of intense frustration looking at disposable plates online, we decided that either we were going to have the wedding we wanted or none at all and elope. We had been so caught up in trying to make the budget work that we had not properly engaged the Universe in manifesting our desires. Recognizing this, we went back to the beginning and started over, very consciously involving Spirit in the entire process.

About a week later, my wife was on a business trip in Northern California, a six-hour drive from where we lived in the Los Angeles area. There were hundreds of people at this particular seminar and my wife (Cheri) struck up a conversation with one of them.

It turns out that this woman was also in the process of planning a wedding and had recently looked at an all-inclusive wedding venue in the L.A. area. This is the first synchronicity. Out of a group of hundreds of people, gathered nearly 400 miles away from where we live, Cheri happened to talk to the one person who had just checked out a wedding venue in our area.

Being all-inclusive, I had my doubts as to the affordability of the location, but we knew we had to check it out, given the seemingly miraculous nature of how this venue came into our awareness. We already had our date selected, and we had already decided on exploring daytime weddings instead of nighttime weddings as a way to save on costs. We called the venue and gave them our wedding date to see if it was available. It was, but there was a "problem."

Our wedding date fell on the week that a big arts festival previewed on the grounds. This meant that we would not have free roam of the entire area (which we never would have used anyway) and that they could only do daytime weddings. But, in order to make up for the "inconvenience" their prices for that week were cut almost in half!

So, because they could only do a wedding when we wanted our wedding, they cut their prices so significantly that we could afford their fee. AND, after the wedding, the only way to leave the venue was through the arts festival, so our wedding guests got free admission to the festival – BONUS!

The wedding venue handled the food, the cake, the table linens, the decorations, the beverages, and came with two day-of coordinators. All we had to do was provide our personal flowers and those for the wedding party. Everything else was done in one swoop for EXACTLY our budget.

The synchronicities of how all of this came together are too "out there" to be anything other than Spirit at work. We had put forth plenty of effort to plan our wedding on our own, but were so focused on what we thought we could afford that we didn't allow room for Spirit's assistance. This resulted in frustration.

There is no way Cheri could have known just who the "right person" was to talk to in order to get the recommendation. We selected our wedding date and decided on a daytime wedding before we ever knew this venue existed, so there is no way we could have planned how great everything worked out. Only the Universe can make connections like that happen. It will make those connections happen for you as well, to the degree you engage it and are open to receiving.

## Visualization Is Not Necessarily "Visual"

Before going into the specific techniques for visualization and some of the tools that can be used in conjunction with the practice of visualization to aid in manifesting your desires, there is one thing to clear up.

Visualization has the word "visual" in it. When talking about visualization, the words "image, picture, see, etc." are often used. This can cause confusion and result in thinking that, in order to "do it right" you must actually see something. This is not the case. Some people, when they visualize, get a clear image in their mind, just like looking at a photograph, and some do not. I am one of those that do not.

On occasion when I am in the practice of visualization I will get something of an actual image, but more often than not I don't. Most of the time, when I visualize, I just get a "sense" of what I am visualizing.

If you are able to get actual images, great! If not, great! Images are not required. I can close my eyes, visualize my wife and me at a café in France, and describe it in exquisite detail, even though all I am "seeing" is the reddish blackness of the backs of my eyelids.

## How to Visualize

There are two primary types of visualization. The first of these is very active and is generally what is meant by the term "visualization." The second type is passive and referred to as "visioning." Both are powerful tools and both take practice, though visualization is generally easier than visioning.

**Visualization:** In Visualization, rather than receiving from the Universe, you are telling the Universe what you want. You're doing your very best to see and feel yourself as already in the experience you are trying to manifest.

This is a very creative process. You're generating the images. You're generating feelings. The more you engage in visualization, the more your vision for what you think is possible will expand.

As you visualize what you're intending to manifest, it becomes more real to your conscious and sub-conscious mind. The more real it becomes, the more you are able to play around and explore in your own vision. As you explore your vision you discover more of what is possible.

There really is no process of Visualization. You just do it and have fun with it. The more clearly you can see, feel, hear, smell, taste, and experience your visualization the more powerful it will be. Once again, your experience in Visualization may be one with vivid, picture-like images or your "seeing" may be more perceptive than literal. The same holds true for feeling, hearing, smelling, and tasting. The way you do Visualization is perfect for you. Period.

**Visioning:** Visioning is a very meditative process. The goal of Visioning is to open yourself up to receive guidance regarding a situation or desire you're working on manifesting.

Visioning is a great place to start if you want to get some more clarity before moving into a deeper manifestation process. Often times, if the goal is somewhat nebulous, Visioning can help to solidify it.

Visioning requires quiet, paper and a pen or pencil, and a willingness to receive new ideas and greater understanding. It is very much a process that requires your surrendering of pre-conceived ideas.

The process begins with a prayer and some time spent in meditation. This helps to set the tone for the Visioning, quiet your internal dialogue, and open your awareness to your intuition. The prayer is to set the intention for the process. There is no prescribed amount of time of meditation required; however enough time should be spent in meditative practices to feel calm, centered, peaceful, and open. After meditation, the visioner asks several questions and remains open to receive answers.

To whom are the questions asked? Who is expected to answer? The visioner can choose to ask their questions and receive their answers from their High Self or Soul, from their intuition, their inner knowing, or even go direct to Spirit. Which you choose doesn't matter so long as you are comfortable asking of and receiving from the source you choose.

The questions asked in a Visioning process can be whatever the visioner chooses, however there are several general questions that are wise to begin with. These questions are:

1. What is Spirit's Highest Vision for...(whatever is the subject of the Visioning)
2. What must I become to empower this vision?
3. What must be released?
4. What must be embraced?
5. Is there any other information that is needed in this moment?

These questions are broad on purpose. Remember, the intention is to receive guidance. By keeping the questions broad, you will tend to remain more open to receiving guidance in whatever way it comes. Once answers to these questions are received, you can go back and ask follow-up questions to clarify what you have already received.

The goal is to remain in as meditative a state as possible so as to remain as open as possible to receive guidance. As such, it is best for the process to take place next to a writing surface and to have the paper and pen/pencil at hand. After each question is asked (internally or out loud, the choice is yours) the visioner returns to the meditative silence and listens inwardly to see what presents itself.

As things come forward, they are allowed to flow from the meditative awareness, down the arm and on to the paper with as little attachment as possible. The less attached you are to what is received, the more open you will remain to receiving. By writing down what comes to you, you don't have to worry about remembering it, which would take you out of the experience.

The information received in a Visioning process can come in really any form at all. You may receive an image or hear a word. You might get a particular feeling in your body, or sense a particular smell. Whatever you receive, do not judge it and do not hold on to it. Let it flow onto the paper and out of your awareness. After the process is complete, you can go back and review your notes.

Whatever you receive (whether you understand it or not) is perfect. It may not make any sense now, but it likely will along the way.

What if you don't get anything from a particular question? No worries. You may not. That's okay. You might have a thought pop into your awareness days later that is the perfect answer to the question. You might never receive an answer. Either way, it does not matter. The only thing that matters is that the process is undertaken with the intention to receive whatever is available to you, for the Highest Good.

After all of the questions have been asked and the visioner feels complete with the process, it is closed with a prayer of gratitude.

If this process fails miserably at your first attempt, do your very best to not get discouraged. Listening to the *still small voice within* takes a lot of practice and attunement. Over time and with practice, it becomes easier to hear.

Your attunement might not be the reason you don't seem to receive anything. The intention of receiving whatever is available to you for your Highest Good includes the possibility of receiving nothing at all. Often times, simply doing the practice, and receiving nothing, is exactly what is needed to set things in motion.

The following is a sample of an opening and closing prayer for a Visioning process. For me, it works best to have the prayer bookends of the process be part of the same Treatment or Affirmative Prayer. The first three steps of the prayer open the Visioning process and the final two close it, with the Visioning itself being a part of the third step. Of course, you should feel free to do this in whatever way works for you.

## Sample Opening Prayer for Visioning

***Recognition:*** *There is only One. One Life. One Mind. One Wisdom. One Intelligence. One Knowing. This One is God, Spirit, the I Am that I Am. It is perfect knowing.*

***Unification:*** *I am one with this One. The Life of Spirit is my life. That which I call my mind, is a part of the Divine Mind of Spirit. My wisdom is God's Wisdom. My intelligence is God's Intelligence. All that I know is part of Spirit's Knowing first.*

***Realization:*** *I now open myself completely to this Divine Mind, this perfect Intelligence. I open myself fully to receive from my own intuition, from the Knowing of Spirit, guidance. In this time, in this Visioning process, as I am one with Divine Mind I know that I will receive from that One Divine Mind exactly what I need to know. I will receive everything that is present and available for me to know, for the Highest Good of myself and all concerned...*

## Sample Closing Prayer for Visioning

***Thanksgiving:*** *I am so grateful for this time of conscious communion with my High Self, with my Intuition, with Spirit. I am filled with gratitude for all that I have received in this process and all that I have not received, for I know that the Highest Good is my ever-present intention. I know that every part of this process was perfect. Thank you.*

***Release:*** *It is done. And So It Is!*

## Tools for Manifestation

A discussion about visualization without some deeper discussion of some tools for manifestation would be incomplete. Visualization alone will not bring about manifestations in your life. There is more to the process. However, before we explore those tools I would like to address a very common misconception about the purpose of manifesting things into your experience.

There is the misconception that the purpose of manifesting "things" is to get "things," and this is not the case. The things you manifest are the icing on the cake. The cake is the consciousness that is built from successfully manifesting your desires.

Things come and things go. Cars, houses, money, jobs, even relationships are temporary. They are tied to the physical and once this physical expression goes away, so do all the things. What doesn't go away is the consciousness you create through manifesting those things.

For example, I have manifested a wonderful marriage with an amazing woman. However, at some point the Soul that is the true nature of who and what I am, will leave this physical body and "Ben Jamison" will be no more. The physical marriage will be over, but all that I learn about love will forever remain with me. When this body dies, all the money I will manifest throughout my lifetime will no longer be mine. However, the consciousness of wealth, prosperity, and abundance that I develop will always be mine.

Don't get me wrong, things can be very nice. As expressions of Spirit, we have the authority to use the creative process to manifest anything we desire (so long as it harms no one, brings more life, and is something we would want for everybody).

> "*Wisdom is the principal thing; therefore get wisdom: and with all thy getting get understanding.*" (Proverbs 4:7)

It is wisdom and understanding we are after, not parking places and cars. If you get confused and think the use of your creative capacity is just to get "stuff" then you will cut yourself off from the real benefit of your ability to manifest.

Greater still is the awareness of your connection to Spirit that the process of manifestation builds. If you come from this perspective, the "thing" you manifest is nice and the consciousness of that "thing" is nicer, but the awareness that you are connected to Spirit and a real, physical world example of that connection is truly the goal. The more you anchor your awareness of that connection in your consciousness, the easier it will be to draw upon it in the future, no matter how difficult your circumstances may be.

The story I previously told of planning my wedding illustrates this perfectly. The "thing" my wife and I were manifesting was the wedding itself. Manifesting our perfect wedding helped to grow our consciousness around abundance, wealth, and love. Yet, over all of that, we now have an exceptionally powerful example of Spirit working through us that we can use as a touchstone in difficult times to remind ourselves that Spirit really is right where we are, hearing our prayers and answering them. The more of these experiences we accumulate, the easier our manifestation efforts will become, as they are done on the foundation of these experiences.

## Practices for Manifestation

All things in spirituality are cyclical and the tools and techniques that can be used in manifestation are the same. While it is completely possible to manifest something right away, do not be surprised or discouraged if it takes time and repeated effort to manifest your desires.

As with everything related to spirituality, including the intention "this or something even better for the Highest Good of all concerned" is vital to the success of your manifestation work. This can be seen from two different perspectives.

Have you ever wished you had something that you didn't get, and later on were glad you didn't actually get what you thought you wanted? We have all had the experience of "buyer's remorse" where shortly after purchasing an item you thought you really wanted, you wish you hadn't.

Buyer's remorse doesn't apply just to things purchased, but can pop up in accomplishments as well, where after working so hard to achieve something, the achievement hardly feels worth the effort. "This or something better...," when used as your standard operating procedure, helps to avoid buyer's remorse, or getting what you asked for even though it wasn't what you thought you were asking for.

The other perspective from which "this or something better..." makes a whole lot of sense is that our best imagination pales in comparison to Spirit's ability to fulfill our desires. Holding the attitude of "this or something better...," leaves room for Spirit to take what you think is possible and make it even better.

## How The Law of Attraction Really Works

The process of manifestation requires far more than just visualization. Pop-spirituality talks about the Law of Attraction and seems to indicate that visualizing or making a vision board[1] and looking at it every day will magically cause all of your worldly desires to fall at your feet. This is not the case.

The Law of Attraction is a Spiritual Law which states that you draw to yourself that for which you are a match. If you want a particular level of car, you must establish the energetic vibration for that type of car within yourself before you can have it.

The simplest example of this is that of voltage in electricity. If you somehow managed to connect a clothes dryer (which operates on 220 volts) to a standard household outlet (110 volts), it wouldn't work because it isn't an energetic match.

This gets much subtler when related to manifestation. Your consciousness establishes your energetic vibration. That vibration dictates what you can and can't have in your life. Your consciousness can be changed and so can your energetic vibration.

Hypothetically speaking (and this is a gross over-simplification), if your energetic vibration is an 8, you will find yourself with cars that match an 8 vibration, friendships that match an 8 vibration, living spaces that match an 8 vibration, etc.

If Ed, vibrating at 8, buys a car vibrating at 15, something will likely happen to cause Ed to lose the car, or the car will be damaged in some way to bring its vibration down to 8. This is why many lottery winners do not remain wealthy for long. They have not increased their consciousness to

1 A vision board is a collage of images that symbolize what you want to manifest.

174

the point where it is an energetic match for many millions of dollars and so those dollars go away.

Once you have established that energetic match within yourself the things you desire are drawn to you. From this perspective it is easy to fall into the idea that visualization-type work is all that is required to activate this Law.

Let's continue with the example of the lottery. A person can do all the inner work necessary to establish the energetic match within themselves of "lottery jackpot winner" but if they never go and buy a ticket, what does it matter? Some people may argue that if you truly have established that energetic match then perhaps a friend will feel the urge to buy you a lottery ticket and give it to you. While it is very true that this may happen, common sense says to go buy the lottery ticket.

I have established within myself the energetic match for clean teeth, and I brush my own teeth. I don't wait for somebody to show up and say "for some reason I really feel called to brush your teeth for you." That example likely comes across as over the top, but it is no more farfetched than the idea that looking at a picture of a house alone will bring you that, or a similar, house. Manifestation requires action and it requires personal responsibility.

## The Living Vision

One of the first tools to create when undertaking a process of manifestation is a *Living Vision* of what you are intending to create. The *Living Vision* is basically a list of the various aspects of what you are intending to manifest that can be used as a reference point. Manifestation requires action on your part and the *Living Vision* helps you to determine what actions to take and how to evaluate the results of your actions.

The *Living Vision* is not a stagnant document, it is living. As you take actions and get results from those actions, your *Living Vision* may well change. Just like with the process of visualization, as you take action toward the manifestation of your desires, those desires are likely to expand and morph into something slightly different, or even something completely different.

First and foremost, the *Living Vision* must contain, actually written out, "this or something better for the Highest Good of all concerned." The importance of this statement in everything to do with spirituality (and even life in general) cannot be overstated.

You can create anything you desire, even things that could make your life more difficult than it needs to be. The good news is that even if you do accidently create something you don't want, there is the potential for benefit from your creation in that you can learn from it. Starting your *Living Vision* with this statement, really meaning it, and keeping it forefront in all you do, will go a long way in helping to make sure you aren't creating more difficulty for yourself.

Aside from the "this or something better..." statement, there are two components to the *Living Vision*. The first of these are the physical aspects of that which you are intending to manifest. If you want a new place to live, what does it look like? Is it an apartment, a duplex, or a house? Do you want to rent or buy? Is central air conditioning a hard and fast requirement or just something that would be very nice, but isn't a deal-breaker?

It's obvious why these types of details are important. It would be a waste of time to look at places that don't come with a dishwasher if a dishwasher is a "must have" for you.

Be ready for these to change throughout the manifestation process. Even the "must have's" may become less important. As the *Living Vision* changes it becomes more aligned with what it is that you really do want, instead of what you *think* you want.

The second component, and the more important component of the two, is the quality component. What are the qualities that are most important to you? Do you want your new home to have the quality of calmness or excitement? How do you want it to feel?

Qualities help like physical aspects do. If you desire solitude, then an apartment building where residents often hang out together in common areas would not be for you.

Qualities also help in allowing your *Living Vision* to expand. Spirit deals far more in qualities than in physical aspects and can bring in more customization for you when your primary focus is on qualities.

I would like to share with you how this expansion of the *Living Vision* might happen, in an example from my life. My wife and I needed a car. We got clear on the physical aspects (four doors, not two, etc.) and we got clear on the qualities we wanted as well. One of those qualities was luxury. The quality of luxury is vastly different than the physical world label of "luxury car." Luxury is a feeling. A luxury car is a label placed on a car to charge a premium for it.

We were totally open to a luxury car that was within our budget, but the quality of luxury was far more important. We were also aware of what physical aspects represented the quality of luxury for us. Heated seats, for example, feel very luxurious to my wife.

However, those physical aspects remained secondary to the quality of luxury. We were open to discovering new physical aspects that feel luxurious to us of which we were not previously aware.

When we found the car that was to be our new car, the quality of luxury was all over it, in ways we expected and in ways we didn't. My wife got her heated leather seats. I got my alloy wheels. Spirit took our desire for the quality of luxury and fulfilled it in ways we had no idea were possible.

The color of the car felt luxurious. We had never considered that one color would feel more luxurious than another. The alloy wheels were designed in a way that felt more luxurious than most alloy wheels. Nowhere on our *Living Vision* nor in our conscious awareness was a Bluetooth system integrated into the car we wanted, yet this car had Bluetooth connectivity integrated into it, which to us feels very luxurious. There is far more expansion to be had when our focus is on qualities rather than physical characteristics.

Once you create your *Living Vision,* review it often. This helps to train your subconscious mind what to be on the lookout for. Frequent review also provides the opportunity for updates.

While updating the *Living Vision* is important, it is also important that the updates be made very consciously and not willy-nilly. Perhaps when somebody first wrote the living vision for their new car, the color blue seemed very important. As they reviewed their *Living Vision* however, they begin to find that while they do like the color blue, it isn't really as important to them as they originally thought. Thus, the color blue stays on the *Living Vision* but it's removed from the list of "must have's." If instead, this person went from blue as a "must have" one day, to red the next, and then black three days later, the process of manifestation will be stunted.

It is also helpful to write a version of the *Living Vision* that is done as affirmations, rather than just a list of ideas. Perhaps the list-style version has the quality of luxury listed. The affirmation-style version, instead of just the word "luxury," may say something like, "I feel luxurious every time I walk up to my car." This version can be reviewed as often as you like, though at least daily is recommended. Reading these affirmations will help to make what you are intending to manifest seem more real and help to speed up the process of aligning your energetic vibration to your desire.

## Creating a Living Vision

As indicated above, there can be many forms of a *Living Vision*, all of which can be useful. The most basic form is simply a list of the qualities and physical descriptions that you're seeking. Begin at the top of a sheet of paper by writing down the thing that you are creating the *Living Vision* for. At the bottom of the page, write the words "this or something better for the Highest Good of all concerned." In between the top and bottom of the page, list what you want. Focus primarily on qualities, but also include physical attributes as well. The items you list can be one word or a short description. In this simplest form of the *Living Vision*, the purpose is to have a quick and easy reference point to remind you of what you really want.

For a more detailed version, begin again with the same page setup on the top and bottom of the page but this time, write your desires in affirmation form. The list created in the simple form of the *Living Vision* is the perfect reference point for creating your affirmations list.

As you go deeper with your *Living Vision* by transforming your list into affirmations, you may find that your list needs updating. Perhaps something that you thought you wanted doesn't feel quite right when you are transforming it into an affirmation or perhaps a quality comes forward in an affirmation that is not on the list. Allow these two formats to influence each other.

You could even create a vision board to be part of your *Living Vision*. As alluded to briefly, a vision board is a collage of words and images that visually symbolize what you are intending to create. You can pull pictures and phrases from magazines, cutting out the portions that reflect your intention. Be sure to include the words "this or something better for the Highest Good of all concerned" on your vision board.

Also, it is vital that pictures of you and those involved be present on your vision board. If you are creating a vision board for a new house, have pictures of everybody who will be living in the house somewhere on the vision board. Vision boards are very creative and artistic, so just allow your creative side to play. Keep the vision board, if you decide to create one, somewhere that you will regularly see it.

## Taking Action

In order to manifest anything, we must take decisive action. The actions we take can be either internal or external, but both types of actions are required for successful manifestation.

External actions are those steps you take primarily in the physical world to bring about your desire. An inventor purchasing supplies to build a prototype is an external action, as is building that prototype. Other examples of external actions are test driving the car of your dreams or researching some aspect of your desire so that you have more information about what you're creating.

External actions are vital, of course, but so are internal actions. Internal actions are actions that help to cultivate your feeling that the thing you want to manifest already is. Visualization is an internal action. Affirmative prayer work is an internal action. Checking inside to see what you're feeling around the results of your external actions and working with those feelings is an internal action.

Internal actions are just as important as external actions. If the desire is a certain amount of money, but your belief structure says that you are not worthy of that amount of money, you must address and change your belief structure. This can be done by applying the tools and techniques taught in this book. If you don't believe you can have something, no amount of external action will bring that something to you.

It can be easy to focus primarily on one type of action, sacrificing the other. Avoid this. Sometimes, what is called for in the manifestation process is mainly internal action. Sometimes, it is the external actions that are required. The internal actions will inform your external actions and your external actions will support your internal actions.

While at times you may be called to focus more predominantly on one type of action instead of the other, overall seek for balance. If you find yourself feeling stuck, it may well be an indication to look at the balance of the activities you have been doing. Perhaps you have been more internally focused and you need some physical movement, or vice versa.

## The Two "Ways of Being" in Taking Action

When taking action there are two "ways of being" that will help a great deal in moving the process forward. In all areas of life, the best way to take any action is with high involvement, but low attachment to the results.

**High Involvement:** Being highly involved in the actions you take is the first way of being. If somebody goes to look at a potential new place to live and is texting with friends while getting the tour, this person is not being very highly involved. If instead this person brings a measuring tape and the dimensions of their furniture to measure the space and has their living vision with them, then they are being highly involved in their action.

Being highly involved also includes checking inside frequently. Being aware of the thoughts and feelings that are present while taking an action can provide a wealth of information for you. Checking within will help bring your intuition into play. Being highly involved also indicates to your subconscious and the Universe that you are serious about manifesting your desires.

When my wife and I were working on manifesting a new home in 2013, the location was very important to us. Location is generally important when looking for where to live, but in Los Angeles, where driving 10 miles can take an hour or more, location is extra important. We knew what our favorite area was, but we looked outside of that area as well. Sometimes we looked 15 miles outside of that area. We were very highly involved in the process.

Now, this might seem like our actions, in looking so far from our desired location, were not very focused and purposeful, but they were. We were so intent on finding our perfect place that we were willing to be open to finding a new area that we weren't aware of that might actually be perfect. We were also allowing the process of looking to give us new information to refine our *Living Vision*.

**Low Attachment:** The second way of being to bring into your actions is that of having low attachment to the results. This is generally the more difficult of the two. During our move in 2013, we wanted to move so badly and had been looking for so long that remaining neutral when yet another place wasn't quite right was a challenge. If you get attached to the results of your actions and those actions don't produce the results you want, you'll end up with constriction. Constriction slows down the process of manifestation.

Manifestation in large part is about receiving and the more constricted you are the more difficult it is to receive. An open hand can receive something much easier than a tightly clenched fist. Having low attachment to the results of your actions will help to keep you out of constriction.

A perspective shift can be helpful in staying unattached to the results of your actions. That perspective shift is this: **There is no failure, ever.** If you are unattached from the results of your actions, then they are always successful because they always produce some result.

Every house we looked at produced a result. Generally that result was a refinement of what we wanted. One place we looked at might have had two or three aspects of our *Living Vision* perfectly, but not have several others. This didn't matter. We had an experience of a few aspects being perfectly in place. Those results allowed us to say back to the Universe, "Okay, these three aspects, yes! We like that. Keep those and let's get the rest in better alignment." This type of feedback is vital to the manifestation process. Even though the house wasn't right for us, it provided invaluable feedback.

This perspective can be beneficial in every area of life. We have all heard some variation of the question, "What would you do if you knew you could not fail?" On a small scale, becoming unattached from the results is a way to practice this idea. I can't fail because everything that I do produces a result. If it is not the result I was hoping for, I now have valuable information to adjust my future efforts.

## Refining

The actions you take will provide results. From those results you can refine your *Living Vision* and your actions. You may discover on a test drive that something on your *Living Vision* that you thought would be very nice to have in your new car really doesn't work for you after all. It may be that seeing a particular result encourages you to expand your *Living Vision* to something even greater, something that you were not aware of before you started taking action.

When planning our wedding, at first we thought we wanted an evening wedding. Weddings generally happen later in the day so that the reception happens at night and we were operating under that tradition. As soon as the idea of a daytime wedding occurred to us and we began to explore the idea, we discovered how much better that would work out for us and our guests. Our *Living Vision* was refined to include our wedding happening during the day.

As you get feedback from the actions you take, you can refine how you take action. The popular "definition" of insanity is doing the same thing over and over and over again, but expecting a different result. If the actions you are taking to plan a vacation are not producing the results you want, perhaps the refinement is to research travel agents who have considerably more knowledge, connections, and experience.

Remember, as you continue to visualize and take actions, your *Living Vision* is likely to shift and expand as your consciousness expands. This is a good thing. Take advantage of it and refine as you go along.

## Waiting...

Sometimes things manifest pretty quickly. Sometimes it can take a while. You must be willing to allow the time that is necessary for your desires to manifest. What might seem simple to us may actually be very complex. In our 2013 move, it took six months of actively looking for new places to live before we found our new home. Finding a new place to live may seem relatively simple, but from a broader perspective we can see all that was involved.

The unit of the duplex we moved into had been previously occupied by the owner of the duplex. The owner only vacated the unit because they had purchased a house a few blocks away. Before we could find the perfect place for us, the owner had to decide to buy another property, look for that property, find that property, and go through the entire process of purchasing it. No wonder it took six months for us to find our next home! But all the work we put in before was not wasted. It helped us to refine our vision and it communicated to the Universe how serious we were about not settling for anything less than what we wanted.

If you become frustrated with seemingly slow progress you will constrict energetically and slow down that process even further. There is no way to know what has to be moved or adjusted for your desires to manifest, both in the external world and your belief system. It could be a whole lot of pieces shifting in the physical world, or it may be one big system of belief within you that needs to be released.

If you're patient and allow the Universe to turn, as it does just fine all on its own, the pieces will fall into place. If you're paying attention to your internal cues along the manifestation process and are engaged in your spiritual practice, the belief systems that need changing will be changed, all in perfect, divine timing.

In *A Course in Miracles* it says that "...infinite patience produces immediate effects." When you truly release your desired timing and allow things to work out in Spirit's timing, you move into this experience of infinite patience.

Now, this quote doesn't indicate that if you want a new car and have infinite patience in getting the car that it will automatically pop up in front of you. The immediate effects produced by infinite patience are peace and receptivity.

If you are infinitely patient, you are not worried or stressed. You are in the state of allowing. From this state

185

you'll be more receptive, not only to receiving that which you desire to manifest, but the intuitive guidance on what actions need to be taken for the manifestation to happen.

When it comes down to it, nothing will happen that is not in perfect timing anyway. No matter how hard you try or how bad you want something to happen on your timeline, it will not happen if the divine timing is not right. Always, there is far more involved in manifesting your desires than you realize and much of that is not done directly by you.

A lock will not open until all the tumblers are in place and nothing you seek to manifest will come to be until all the cosmic tumblers have aligned. Having your desired timeline is just fine. In fact, it is essential for providing context to your desires. Vital also is your willingness to, regardless of your timelines, open to divine timing.

## Gratitude and Celebration

If you remain aware during your efforts to manifest something, you'll begin to see different pieces start to fall into place. When they do, gratitude and celebration is called for. No matter how seemingly small the event, it is wise to take time to acknowledge the success and celebrate it. Gratitude is one of the most powerful tools available to open up your willingness to receive.

The celebration doesn't have to be something extravagant. When my wife and I finally found our wedding venue, our celebration was to stop on our way back into work at a Starbucks to share a vanilla latte and biscotti. Your celebration can be as simple as a quiet, "Yes!" to yourself. It can also be as extravagant as you want.

Of course, another aspect of this is that being aware of making progress encourages more progress. It helps to build the internal feeling of momentum. Throw some gratitude on that momentum and it's like throwing gas on a fire...though not nearly as dangerous.

Once your desire has been manifested, gratitude, gratitude, gratitude! Express gratitude to Spirit for the manifestation. Express gratitude to yourself for all the effort you put in as well. This gratitude will help anchor your accomplishment into your consciousness.

Remember, in manifesting "stuff" what we are really going for is the increased faith in and awareness of your ever-present connection to Spirit. Your ability to partner with the Universe and manifest something is far more important than the thing you manifest. Gratitude and celebration can help to bring this more powerfully and concretely into your awareness.

## How Visualization and Manifestation Help Bring Complete Emancipation from All Discord of Every Nature

Visualization and manifestation help to build up your faith. As you rack up experiences of successful manifestation, your faith and your reliance on that faith tend to increase. The purpose of manifestation is to build your consciousness of Spirit's ever-presence in your life. The more examples of this you have the more capable you will be of remaining in a neutral, faith-based place when difficult circumstances arise.

If you live in the awareness that Spirit is always working with and through you, then an experience that would otherwise have thrown you into strife and discord will not shake your peace or calm repose. This is a high goal to reach, but it is reachable. Along the way to reaching that goal, you'll find that the experiences of discord are shorter and less intense than they used to be.

Through the process of Visioning you can begin to build your awareness of your connection to Spirit. The truth is that you are not now, nor ever were, nor ever will be, separated from Spirit. Spirit is all there is. It is impossible to be disconnected from that which is everything. It is your awareness of that connection that needs cultivating and Visioning is a powerful tool to help build that awareness.

The more you practice asking into Spirit and listening back, the more present in your life that connection will be. Ultimately, you'll be able to ask into Spirit, "What is Spirit's highest intention for this situation," and receive an immediate and direct answer. As you practice Visioning, your growing awareness of your connection to Spirit will help you to navigate troubled waters more gracefully.

Visualization and manifestation also help your life to work better. The more you visualize your desires, the clearer the Universe is on what to put in front of you. The more you manifest, when intending "this or something better..." the more harmonized the things in your life will be. These practices also bring to the surface beliefs that are in the way of your manifestation efforts in order for you to change them. As more and more of your limiting beliefs are released, the better your life will work. As life works better, there is less discord.

## Treatment regarding Visualization and Manifestation

*Recognition:* *There is only one Life. This Life is perfect. This Life is the Perfect Life of God. This Life is creative. It manifests all that there is through It's vision.*

*Unification:* *I am one with this Life. It is the Life that I live and It is present with me, in me, as me. As part of this Divine Whole I have access to perfect manifestation and perfect vision. I am* creative and have the ability to call into action the laws of creation and use them for my Highest Good.

**Realization:** *I am an expression of the Divine. I have within me the capacity for visualization, perfect visualization. I am able to visualize my desires and, through decisive action, manifest them.*

*The way I experience the practice of visualization is perfect, for I am the only one who can visualize the way that I do.*

*I am open to receive inspiration and intuition from my visualization and my visioning.*

*As I take action toward the manifestation of my desires I remain highly involved and have low attachment to the results for I know that every result brings me closer to my dreams.*

*I celebrate every time another piece comes into place as I recognize my forward progress and flood the Universe and myself with gratitude every time I move closer to my goal.*

*I remain open to new and expanded ideas, allowing my vision to grow and change as it becomes more and more aligned with Spirit. My spiritual practice supports me in this process as I use it to clear old patterns and beliefs that no longer serve me.*

*Above all, I hold to the intention that my desires, or something even better for the Highest Good of all concerned are being done with Spirit, through me. I know that the true purpose of visualization and manifestation is to bring me into greater alignment with Spirit and to anchor in my conscious awareness my ever-present connection with God.*

***Thanksgiving:*** *I am so grateful for my ability to visualize, vision, and manifest. Thankful feelings pour forth from every bit of my being for the knowing that all my efforts are inspired by and infused with Spirit and that the Universe always conspires for my Highest Good.*

***Release:*** *I now release this prayer into the Universe. It has already been received and the answer is already "Yes." I claim it good, and very good. It is done. AND SO IT IS!*

# Chapter Fourteen

## Spirtual Practice: Forgiveness

The practice of forgiveness has amazing power to improve your life. There are countless stories of miracles happening in people's lives around forgiveness work. Take Nelson Mandela for example. Rather than hold judgments against the people who imprisoned him for 27 years, he found forgiveness in his heart and changed his country and the world. An act of complete forgiveness opened Wayne Dyer up to receive the divine inspiration to write over 30 books.

Seemingly miraculous experiences are available to all of us, if we are willing to forgive, which can sometimes be very difficult to do. This in part is due to how society typically understands forgiveness, which is incorrect. By the end of this chapter, you will have a new understanding of what forgiveness means and how to do it. This new understanding will not only make it easier to come by the willingness to forgive, but will actually help excite you about doing forgiveness work.

The standard idea of forgiveness in our society is that we forgive people for something bad they have done. While this can be an important step on the way to actual forgiveness, it is not the end and, in fact, is not even required.

One of my favorite definitions of forgiveness comes from the book *Unconditional Love and Forgiveness* by Edith R. Stauffer, Ph.D.

> *"To forgive is to cancel all demands, conditions, and expectations held in your mind that block the Attitude of Love; that is to say, to cancel the conditions, demands, and expectations which prevent the mind from maintaining the Attitude of Love."*

In other words, forgiveness is the process by which you return to your experience of love. All of the "conditions, demands, and expectations" can be boiled down into just one word – judgment. There is a tremendous amount of energy locked up in judgment. The process of forgiveness frees up that energy. Often times, this freeing of energy is described as a weight being lifted, which is a really good description because judgments carry surprising emotional weight.

Forgiveness returns you to your experience of love, which is being blocked by the judgments you hold. Remember from the chapter on Love that love is your true essence, your true nature. To use a metaphor from nature, let's look at water. Water's nature is to flow. Your nature is to love. Water can be stopped from flowing by building a dam. You can block your experience of your loving nature by holding judgments.

There is tremendous pressure behind a dam. At the base of the Hoover Dam, for example, 45,000 pounds of pressure per square foot can be withstood. It takes extreme energy to hold ourselves as cut off from our true nature of love. Once a judgment is released through forgiveness, all of the energy that was holding it in place is freed up.

# The Nature of Judgment

It is commonly accepted, from the spiritual perspective, that judgments are not great to have. John-Roger has a wonderful, and in my opinion accurate way of describing judgment. He says, "Judgment is the poison we take hoping somebody else will die." This may sound harsh and out of proportion with reality at first, but when explored deeper, the truth of this statement becomes clear.

Scientific studies have shown that a five-minute experience of anger (which is a symptom of judgment) can suppress the immune system for up to six hours. Suppression of the immune system sure sounds like poisoning to me, and it is something we do to ourselves. Even if a judgment is not activated as anger in your experience in the moment, that judgment is still with you (until you forgive and release it) waiting to flare up.

There is but one cause for every judgment anybody has ever made and ever will make: lack of acceptance. As discussed earlier, "acceptance is the first law of spirit." When you are not in acceptance of what is, you have taken yourself out of harmony with one of the most basic and fundamental Laws of the Universe.

Remember, acceptance does not mean that you just give up and take whatever comes your way. When you are in acceptance you evaluate the circumstances and act accordingly. When you are not in acceptance you judge, and as a result, unconsciously cut yourself off from your true nature of loving, bind up your energy in self-destructive emotions and lose a great deal of your ability to act from a place of inner empowerment.

# The Nature of Forgiveness

Forgiveness brings you back into alignment with acceptance. It frees the energy you had locked away, opens you back up to the Love that you truly are, and brings you to a place where you can take powerful and effective action.

I mentioned earlier that the typical idea of forgiveness is that we forgive somebody for something they have done. If Sue keyed your car, for example, the standard idea of forgiveness would be to walk up to Sue and say "I forgive you for keying my car." This may be very helpful and healing but it falls short because there is still judgment present.

Another example makes this clearer. Math. Yes, the example is math - again. You may be a mathematician. You may understand math. Math is not a language that I speak well. Frequently, while doing math homework, I would say (sometimes quite loudly) "This is so stupid!" So, if I were to take that phrase and do the traditional idea of forgiveness I would say to math, "I forgive you, Math, for being stupid." That statement makes no sense. Math is not stupid. Math is math. I judged math as being stupid. The forgiveness work is not related at all to math, but to my judgments about math.

Looking back at the example of Sue from this perspective, the forgiveness work that is truly needed is in forgiving my judgments of Sue and her actions. I may forgive Sue for doing what she did, but my judgments about what she did still remain. In fact, forgiving Sue for her actions is not even necessary if you are able to forgive your judgments about her actions. This would sound something like "I forgive myself for judging Sue's keying of my car as very inconsiderate."

This can be a tall order in some situations. It may well require that you find forgiveness within yourself for the action before you can come to a place of being able to forgive the judgment. If so, by all means, forgive actions and people every time you need to. Just don't stop there. Go beyond. Identify and forgive the judgments themselves.

A key word in the practice of forgiveness (forgiveness work) to let you know that you have not yet arrived at the meat of the judgment is the word "being." If I were to say, "I forgive Edward for being a jerk," that does not get to the judgment. The judgment is that Edward is a jerk. Therefore, the appropriate forgiveness phrase would be "I forgive myself for judging Edward as a jerk."

You may have noticed that the phrasing I'm using to indicate that forgiveness is being done on the deepest level possible is "I forgive *myself for judging...*" You see, when it comes right down to it, the only way to get all of the judgment cleared is to recognize that we made the judgment and the only person to forgive is our self for having ever judged in the first place.

## The Process and Practice of Forgiveness

Too often somebody will say something like "You really ought to forgive *blah, blah, blah*," without any instruction on how to actually do forgiveness work. Rest assured, this book will not leave you hanging. There are several techniques available in forgiveness work. I will share two of them with you here. Both of them are effective on their own and work wonderfully in conjunction as well. Before we get to them, however, there is one more thing about the traditional idea of forgiveness that needs to be eliminated.

No conversation with anybody is required for forgiveness to take place. Forgiveness work doesn't require anybody but you. In fact, it is something best done with, for, and by yourself. This is very good news, especially if you're holding judgments related to people who are no longer alive. Plus, trying to do forgiveness work with the person around whom you hold judgments could make things more difficult. Walking up to somebody and saying, "I forgive you for being such a jerk to me" is not likely to do either of you any good. Saying "I forgive myself for judging you as a jerk" to that person won't help either.

Furthermore, remember that what is really being forgiven is not a person or an action, but rather our judgments about the person or the action. The judgment takes place 100% inside of us and can only be forgiven and cleared inside of us.

## Forgiveness Technique – Long Form

This technique for forgiveness was taught to me by the Rev. Dr. Harry Morgan Moses. This form of forgiveness can be done on your own, or with a trained facilitator.

**DISCLAIMER:** I strongly encourage you to NOT facilitate somebody else through this process without significantly more training than this book offers. It is absolutely fine to work the process through by yourself, as the judgments and energy contained within them are yours already. Facilitating others in forgiveness work carries with it the potential for energetic entanglement with other people's judgments and energies, which can be detrimental to both the facilitator and the person doing the forgiveness work. It takes significant study and training to be able to remain energetically clear while facilitating this type of work, and to help direct somebody through the deep feelings that can be brought forward. If being a forgiveness facilitator appeals to you, I strongly encourage you to find a qualified instructor to work with.

This long form forgiveness technique requires two chairs, paper, and a pen. Set the two chairs facing each other, as if two people were to sit across from each other. You will sit in one of the chairs and the other chair will remain physically unoccupied.

**Step 1:** *Begin by doing an affirmative prayer, asking for Spirit's guidance throughout the forgiveness work. As always, be sure to include* "for the Highest Good of all concerned." *You can do a full 5-step affirmative prayer, or break the prayer up, as described in the Visioning process, to book-end your forgiveness work. Forgiveness work is very sacred. Attuning to the Divine, and calling in Spirit will be quite beneficial to the process.*

**Step 2:** *Close your eyes and bring to mind the person or situation you want to forgive. Remember, the forgiveness is not of the person as such, but your judgments around the person, their actions, or the situation. Visualize this person sitting in the other chair.*

**Step 3:** *Speak to this person. Say something along the lines of* "I need to do forgiveness work around you, (name). I have judged (you / this situation / myself / whatever is present). I have been carrying these judgments for (how long you have been carrying them) and I am ready and willing to forgive."

**Step 4:** *Bring to mind all of the judgments you have made about this person, the situation, or yourself. Write them down. The format goes like this...* "I judged _____ as _____." *If need be, the "as" can be replaced with "for," however do not leave it there. Follow it up with an "as" judgment. Here is an example.* "I judged Bill **for** breaking the window. And, I judged Bill's breaking the window **as** inconsiderate." *This is important because we want to get rid of all the judgments. If we forgive judging Bill **for** something, there is still the judgment tied to* *the action itself. As mentioned before, also be sure that the word* "being" *is not present.*

**Step 5:** *Once you have your list written, speak them out loud to the person you have placed in the other chair.* "I judged _____ as _____."

**Step 6:** *Feel into your body. Where do these judgments reside? What do they feel like? When you have a location and a feeling, speak those out loud to the person you have placed in the other chair.* "I hold these judgments (in my stomach, chest, knees, etc.). They feel (heavy, sticky, dark, or any other descriptor that fits).

**Step 7:** *This step deals with responsibility. Responsibility will be discussed at length in a later chapter, but for now just know that taking responsibility for your actions and releasing misplaced responsibility for the actions of others is very powerful and exceptionally important in forgiveness work.*

*Review the situation in your mind. Write down all of the things that others are responsible for in the situation and all of the things that you are responsible for, keeping separate lists. This may be something like* "Bill is responsible for breaking the window. I am responsible for not cleaning up the spill on the floor that Bill slipped on just before he broke the window."

*Once you feel that you have all the responsibilities for the situation in the correct place, review it one more time just to be sure. Then, to the person you have placed in the other chair, say* "I take full responsibility for my actions, and I give you full responsibility for yours."

**Step 8:** *Close your eyes. Recall the place in your body where you hold your judgments and how they feel. Visualize yourself energetically reaching inside, taking hold of those judgments and feelings, and removing them from your body. Bound up in those judgments are the areas where you have, up until now, inappropriately taken responsibility. Physically* *move your hands as you do this. When you have this visualized mass of judgment in your hands, pass it over to the person in the other chair.*

*The other person is not taking your judgments on themselves, but rather is holding the judgments for you momentarily. It is easier to forgive when the judgments are outside of your body. Keep in mind that the responsibility you used to hold for their actions is in that bundle as well. By passing this bundle over to the other person you are symbolically clearing yourself of that over-responsibility.*

**Step 9:** *With the judgments and over-responsibility outside of your body, you will now begin to forgive. Using your list of judgments, one by one, speak a phrase of forgiveness.* "I forgive myself for judging _____ as _____."

*After each statement of forgiveness, find some Truth about the situation to speak in its place. For example, your judgment may be against Sarah. Let's say you judged Sarah as mean. The forgiveness statement would be* "I forgive myself for judging Sarah as mean." *The Truth statement following this might be something like* "The Truth is that Sarah is Spirit, just like I am. The Truth of Spirit is loving and so, at the core of who she is, Sarah is loving also."

*Continue this process – forgiveness statement followed immediately by a Truth statement – until you have completed your entire list.*

**Step 10:** *Feel inside your body. Are more judgments lurking? If so, write them down and repeat Step 9.*

**Step 11:** *Having forgiven all the judgments you are aware of, it is now time to move back into your experience of Love. Remember, your true nature is Love and your judgments block your experience and expression of that Love. Having forgiven those judgments, your experience of Love is available to you once again. Open yourself to this Love and say out loud to the person you have placed in the opposite chair* "I cancel the demands and expectations that have been blocking my experience of love. I love you _____. I want nothing but the Highest Good for you and I release you in my mind and heart to your Highest Good."

**Step 12:** *Visualize, about a foot above your head, a ball of brilliant, pure white Light. This ball of Light begins to pour Light from Its inexhaustible self into the top of your head. This Light flows through your entire body. It cleanses you. It gently and lovingly dissolves any remnants of judgment from you. This Light leaves your body through your feet and circles back around, including the person you have placed in the other chair, before returning to the ball.*

*This represents the Unconditional Love that is the Truth of who you are. This Unconditional Love excludes nobody, no matter what they may or may not have done. From an Unconditionally Loving place, of course you want the other person to be included in your Unconditional Loving, which is why, in the visualization, the Light includes them as it circles back around.*

**Step 13:** *Do a closing prayer.*

**Step 14:** *Celebrate and honor yourself for being willing to enter into this deep level of forgiveness work.*

This process may take 10 minutes and it may take much longer. Make sure before you sit to undertake this forgiveness process that you will have plenty of uninterrupted time to complete the entire process.

## Forgiveness Technique – Short Form

This "short form" of forgiveness is indeed short. In the short form, when you become aware of a judgment operating in your experience, all you do is identify the judgment, center yourself, and say "I forgive myself for judging...." and speak the judgment with the intention of clearing it from your consciousness. This statement should then be followed up with a statement of Truth about the situation. This may be short, but it is not necessarily easy.

Recognizing that you are in an experience of judgment can be tricky. It takes intention and practice to get enough of a space in between your experiences/actions and your conscious awareness of what is going on inside your experience. A daily meditation practice is extremely helpful in training your conscious awareness to observe what you're doing and experiencing, rather than getting caught up in it. Luckily, there is one fail-proof way to know that a judgment is operating. Are you upset? If the answer is "yes" then somewhere in your consciousness a judgment is active.

Once you recognize you are upset, complete the following sentence: I am upset because _____. What you place after the "because" is either the judgment itself or the neon sign pointing to the judgment. For example, "I'm upset because this jerk just cut me off!" The obvious judgment in that statement is that the other driver is a jerk. So, "I forgive myself for judging the other driver as a jerk. The Truth is (pulling from your practice of Loving) the other driver is inherently valuable and, because he/she exists, I send him/her my love."

Let's try a little experiment. First, imagine yourself being cut off in traffic and reacting the way people typically react. Yell and curse. Tell the other driver how horrible and stupid they are. Make sure they get a good view of your middle finger. How do you feel? Next, reset the situation and instead of reacting in the typical fashion, go through the short form of forgiveness in the example above. How different do you feel than when you react in the more traditional way?

Being cut off in traffic and the judgment that flows from that experience tends to be much simpler to handle.

Obviously, for the most part, the long form of forgiveness work is not required for such circumstances and the short form is more than up to the task. But what about deeper, more intense judgments? Can the short form be used for those as well? The answer is yes…sort of.

With more deeply held or complex judgments, the short form of forgiveness work is great as a band-aid. Some aspect of a deeply held judgment may crop up at a place and time where you can't do the long form right away. In that case, the short form can help to relieve the experience of upset. In fact, it will eventually clear the judgment completely, just like the long form will. However, odds are it will take much longer to clear the judgment with the short form alone. The best practice is to use the short form of forgiveness if you are not immediately able to do the long form and then schedule a time to engage in deeper forgiveness work.

## Forgiveness Technique – Create Your Own

There is really no "right" or "wrong" way to do forgiveness. If it works, work it. If it doesn't work for you, change it or find some other practice. You can even create your own way of doing forgiveness as long as it follows a few simple guidelines:

1. Forgiveness work is something you do with, for, and by yourself. Nobody else is required.
2. Forgiveness work is based in love and its intention is to return you to a greater experience of love.
3. Forgiving must ultimately be about the judgments you placed against others (people, actions, events, things, etc.)

# Judge Not, Lest Ye Be Judged

This biblical quote is bandied about quite frequently, but rarely does anybody explain what it actually means. Once it is understood it becomes a wonderful tool to help in forgiveness work – and in staying out of judgment to begin with. In order to explain this quote, let's go back to the example of getting cut off while driving.

Here's the set-up. You are driving down the street on your way to work, minding your own business and obeying traffic laws. Suddenly, somebody speeds up next to you on the right and with barely any room in front of you, cuts you off just barely missing a car parked on the side of the road. You fly into judgment of this person as a terrible driver and get enraged.

You ride up right on their bumper, honking your horn, to let them know how pissed you are. You give them the finger and yell and scream at them. You just became a terrible driver. Tailgating somebody on a busy street is terrible driving. In order to show somebody who you judged as a terrible driver how bad of a driver you think they are, you became just as bad of a driver. Judge not, lest ye be judged. But wait, it gets worse...

All that rage and anger – who is the one experiencing that rage and anger? Is it the other driver? No. It is you. You are the one who gets the experience of the rage and anger and all the negative health consequences that go along with them. If you really think about it – somebody who is in such a rush to drive that way probably isn't really all that concerned with what you think anyway. They aren't waiting around to see if you're upset or not so that, if you are upset, they can get upset too. That rage and anger began in you and it stays with you. Judge not, lest ye be judged...

## Compassion in Forgiveness

The practice of compassion done in conjunction with forgiveness work will quicken you on your way toward forgiving a judgment for the last time.

> *"If we could really know what is in the hearts of our 'enemies,' we would never do another thing to hurt them because there is already enough hurt."*
>
> ~ John-Roger

If we could really know what is in the heart of whomever we are judging, we would instantly cease to judge them. If we could truly understand what it is that causes people to act or react in a certain way we would be overcome with compassion. Unfortunately, the vast majority of the time we're not given to know what is in another person's heart or experience. So you have a choice. You can choose to judge them, or you can choose compassion. Remember, "there but for the grace of God, go I."

Here is another way to look at it. If you or I had the same experiences as the person we are judging, we would likely be doing the exact behaviors for which we are judging them. It is also likely that if you are judging somebody or something, it is because either you do that same thing, have done that same thing, or are afraid that you might do that same thing. "There but for the grace of God, go I."

There is no way to really know why people do the things they do. This means you have a wonderful opportunity to choose what to believe in a way that most supports you. Think back to the example of the driver that cut you off on your way to work. Why did that driver decide to drive that way? You don't know. You can make up a story that they are an inconsiderate jerk and go into judgment.

You can also assume that they are driving the way they are because there is some emergency situation that they are rushing to. If that were the case, would you go into judgment at all? Would you instead give them extra room and send them a blessing? If you are making up a story anyway, you might as well make up a story that brings you into your spiritual practice, rather than one that drop-kicks you into the hell of being in judgment.

Remember, with yourself and with everybody else – we all do the very best we can. If we truly knew better, we would do better. The Truth is always that everybody does their very best with what they know at the time. Recognizing this will speed up your forgiveness work dramatically.

## How Many Times Do I Forgive?

When it comes to the more simple judgments, if you catch them quickly and do the forgiveness work right away, they tend to clear pretty easily. I'm referring to the general "I got cut off in traffic" type of judgments. The more deeply held judgments can tend to take longer, but it is possible to clear them just as quickly.

The Bible quotes Jesus as saying we should forgive "seventy times seven." Unfortunately for people who take the Bible literally, this does not mean that after 490 statements of forgiveness, any judgment is automatically released for sure, forever. If that were the case, this whole thing would be easy. It would take under 15 minutes. Yes, I just looked at a clock and timed myself. I was able to say "I forgive myself for judging myself as unworthy" 10 times in 15 seconds.

In reality, you forgive until the judgment is released. You may be done after one time of the short forgiveness process or it may take many times through the long form.

There is no way to know what it will take ahead of time. And, for the most part, there is no way to tell for sure that the judgment has been forgiven for the last time.

There are some signposts to indicate that what you are doing is working to clear the judgments. Perhaps you will feel an emotional release or a sense of peace wash over you. Perhaps you will notice a change in your behavior. While these things do indicate progress, they do not necessarily indicate completion of the forgiveness work. Forgiveness is an ongoing practice.

While it is possible for a judgment to clear completely, all at once, in a definitive way, this is rarely the case. Forgiveness has happened for me this way just once in the last decade.

I fell out of touch with a person who was once very important to me, because of money. I was owed a sum of money that was not repaid and after a while of my asking for it, this person stopped answering or returning my calls. I went into judgment. For years I had no contact with this person and got pissed every time they entered my thoughts. I did forgiveness work after forgiveness work after forgiveness work with little result.

After many years, I came across this person's Facebook profile. As I looked at it, suddenly and unexpectedly, I felt all the judgment I had been carrying around fall away. In an instant the weight of those judgments was gone and the loving that I had been blocking for all those years flooded back into my experience. It was wonderful. It was so apparent that the judgments were released for the last time. This sudden release of a judgment has happened once for me and it took years of forgiveness work for it to happen that way.

More likely than not, the clearing of judgments will happen gradually. When you begin to work with forgiving a particular judgment, that judgment might pop up for you every day. After a few rounds of forgiveness, you may notice you experience the judgment only three times a week. After more work it might crop up every other week or so.

Then, one day you will look back and realize that it has been several years since that judgment came up in your experience. This is a good indication that the judgment has been fully released. When did it happen? Who knows? Was it released fully and completely? Who knows? It may crop up again, it may not. It just is what it is.

Don't let this frustrate you. If you engage strongly in a practice of forgiveness work, the results in your life will be significant, whether or not you know for sure that a judgment has been completely forgiven.

## How Forgiveness Helps Bring Complete Emancipation from all Discord of Every Nature

Discord in your life comes from your judgments. The spiritual practice of Forgiveness, by clearing those judgments from your consciousness, clears the discord that they bring. As you are liberated from your judgments, so too are you liberated from the experience of discord. Everybody has heard someone describe the experience of having a "weight lifted from my shoulders" and you have likely experienced this yourself as well. Judgments are weighty things. When you release them through forgiveness you feel lighter, more buoyant, and have more energy.

Forgiveness returns to you the experience of love that your judgments have held at bay. The more love you experience, the less discord you experience. Love and discord are not able to co-exist, just like light and dark can't occupy the same space. There is no struggle between the two. Love comes in and discord disappears. The more love you have in your experience, the less likely discord is to be present. If your judgments keep your experience of love away 50% of the time, for that other 50% of the time, you are available for discord. As you clear judgments, the amount of your days that are spent experiencing love increase and the potential time available for discord decreases.

As you begin to delve deeply into a forgiveness practice, you get better and better at it. A judgment that, at the beginning, may take many sessions to forgive will be released much easier as you continue to practice forgiveness. This practicing aligns you with the energies of liberation and freedom.

Eventually, you will have done so much forgiveness work on, for example, getting cut off in traffic, that the judgments won't even come in anymore because liberating yourself from them has become such a default practice that the judgments can't even stick to begin with. Staying out of experiences that bring discord is a great way to emancipate yourself from that discord.

## Treatment regarding Forgiveness

*Recognition:* There is only one Life, one Presence, and one Power. This Life is God, Spirit, the Universe, Love. It is the only Life there is and it is completely, perfectly, unconditionally loving.

*Unification:* I Am that one Life. It is the only Life and therefore is, and must be the Life that I live. I am connected to It, inseparable from It, and Its nature is my nature.

*Realization:* There is no judgment in Spirit. Spirit is Unconditional Love and Unconditional Love does not and cannot judge. It can only Love. This Unconditional Love is also my nature. It *is who and what I am. No matter how I may judge another, my nature is not judgment, but Unconditional Love. As such, the possibility for the forgiveness of my judgments is always present, always available, and always supported and encouraged by the entire Universe.*

*And so, aligning with my true nature, I forgive. I forgive the judgments I have made against others. God is all there is. All "others" are really just God hiding behind a different mask. Everybody always does the very best they believe they can do. Knowing that everybody always does their best, my judgments melt away and the Love that I am returns to me, easily and gracefully.*

*I forgive. I forgive the judgments I have made against myself. I am a beloved child of Life. God does not judge me. No matter what I say, do, feel, or think, God loves me unconditionally. I follow God's example and love myself, releasing any and all judgments into the living Light of Love that is the nature of God and the nature of me.*

*Whether I am forgiving judgments against myself or others, I recognize that God is supporting me in my forgiveness work. I recognize that Spirit is with me, guiding me and encouraging my return to Love. With the entire Universe conspiring with me, my successful forgiveness of every judgment is guaranteed.*

***Thanksgiving:*** *I am so very grateful that Love is who I am. I am so very grateful that I have within me the power to forgive all the judgments I have ever made. I am so very grateful that Spirit supports me in my forgiveness work.*

***Release****: Knowing that this prayer has already been received and answered with a resounding "Yes! This or something even better for the Highest Good of all," I release it into creation. I call it good, and very good. It is done. And So It IS!*

# Chapter Fifteen

# Spirtual Practice: Gratitude

*G*ratitude is a practice you can do intentionally. When you relegate gratitude to an experience that just happens to come upon you when your life seems "good enough" to deserve gratitude, you're missing out. In truth, gratitude is something you can actively experience and a spiritual practice that you can consciously utilize for your upliftment and growth.

The practice of gratitude activates your connection to Spirit in a powerful way. It is an open channel through which you can pull into your life astounding experiences. The practice of gratitude can take any negative experience and, depending on how deeply you engage in your gratitude, completely eliminate it. Through gratitude your vision remains clear. You are better able to see your life as it actually is, rather than through the lens of what is missing from life. It also drastically speeds up the process of manifestation.

## Gratitude in Manifestation

Gratitude quickens manifestation by helping to keep your focus on what you want, rather than what is missing. By looking for opportunities to practice gratitude in the manifestation process, you are focusing your attention on your progress, rather than on your desire not being in your physical experience.

Every time your focus shifts to what is missing, the Universe receives the message that what you want more of is the "missing." The Laws of creation can't interpret what you really want from a focus on what is missing any more than the soil can grow corn from a radish seed. It takes your focus and brings you more of what you're focusing on.

## Gratitude as Thanksgiving

Many people only consciously practice gratitude on the Thanksgiving holiday, however, gratitude as thanksgiving is available to you every day. Gratitude as thanksgiving means simply saying "thank you." There are far more opportunities to say "thank you" than many people ever take advantage of, and often, when "thank you" is said there is a disconnection from the experience of gratitude. It is said simply out of polite habit.

There is no limit to who or what can receive your "thank you." Most generally they are directed toward others who do nice things for us, but you can say "thank you" to nature when the weather is particularly beautiful. You can give your "thank you" to an animal that lets you pet it. You can even say "thank you" to yourself.

That may sound strange, yet it is a wonderful way to experience gratitude. If you have an intuitive feeling that you follow and it turns out to be a wonderful thing, you can say "thank you" to yourself for following that intuition. If you do something out of the ordinary and helpful for somebody else, you don't need to wait for them to express gratitude for your generosity. Nothing says I can't say, "Thank you Ben, for helping that person. I really appreciate about me that my first instinct is so often to help others when I see the need."

## Gratitude as Appreciation

I love looking at the definitions of words and finding a depth of meaning there that is often overlooked. Gratitude is often used interchangeably with the word appreciation. If we look at another meaning for appreciation, we discover that it also means to increase in value. When the value of something appreciates it becomes worth more. The same thing happens with gratitude.

The more gratitude or appreciation you express for somebody or something, the more it will grow in value for you. As this person or thing becomes more valuable to you, the tendency is to appreciate it more, which makes it more valuable in your estimation which is followed by more appreciation. It is a wonderful cycle that you can consciously engage.

Appreciation also implies expansion or growth beyond value. If you truly appreciate somebody and express that appreciation, that person is more likely to enjoy spending time with you. Being appreciated, genuinely appreciated, feels good. We all like to hang out in good vibes. Think about it. If you had two acquaintances, and acquaintance A tended to express gratitude for you in their life more than acquaintance B, which do you think would be more likely to move from acquaintance to friend? Clearly, acquaintance A would be more likely to graduate to friendship.

This is only the case for genuine, heartfelt gratitude however. An expression of gratitude for the purpose of manipulating somebody to spend more time with you is generally seen through pretty quickly. It just doesn't feel quite right. But genuine appreciation will deepen your relationships like nothing else.

There is another interesting thing about expressing gratitude to people and about things in your life. That gratitude becomes yours. As you express your gratitude to other people, they feel that expression of gratitude and are uplifted. But in order to genuinely express gratitude, you must first be in the experience of gratitude. Then, by expressing your gratitude, the appreciation principle is automatically applied to your experience of gratitude and it increases. Gratitude is one of those wonderful things that you get more of the more you give it away.

## Gratitude as Recognition of Something Greater

All of life is interconnected. To quote Rev. Dr. Harry Morgan Moses,

*"There is no such thing as a disconnected anything."*

Everything is connected. Everything in your experience is connected to you. From the spiritual context of life there are no random happenings or experiences.

This means that everything that happens in your experience has purpose and meaning whether you recognize it or not. The Universe is affirmative and expansive. It is Its nature. So, everything that happens in your experience is connected to you, is purposeful, and has within it the possibility of growth and expansion for you. No matter what the experiences in your life are like, the Truth is that through any experience you have the possibility of becoming more than you were without that experience. If you can really embody this perspective you can find an experience of gratitude for *everything* going on in your life.

This is sometimes easy and sometimes very difficult, but no matter how difficult it may seem to find gratitude for an experience, the possibility is there.

If you can find that gratitude another wonderful thing happens: You move through the difficult experiences faster and easier, and, what you learn from those experiences gets anchored and integrated into who you are more powerfully. The wonderful experiences become richer and last longer as well. How gratitude does this with enjoyable experiences is self-evident but how gratitude works with difficult experiences may not be quite so obvious.

Often times in difficult experiences people tend to get trapped into focusing on the "negative" or what is "wrong." This habit is due to societal conditioning. It is the default operating procedure because that is what most people observe in the world. By focusing on what is "wrong," that very thing tends to increase or at the very least stick around. Remember, the Universe is affirmative and expansive. It takes what you focus on and affirms and expands it. This isn't the Universe being mean; it's just what the Universe does. The Universe doesn't deal in good and bad or right and wrong. Those are human definitions. The Universe simply deals with what is.

If you recognize that everything has with it the potential for your learning and growth and you move into gratitude right away, no matter the quality of your experience, you are more likely to stay away from focusing on the negative aspects.

Consider the example of being mugged. If a person who was mugged does not focus on the mugging but rather says, "Okay – I got mugged. That sucked. However, there is something here for me. Even in an experience as intense as this, there is something that I can learn from it. There is some way that I can grow and become a better person because of this, and I am grateful for that," they will likely move through the trauma of the experience quicker, and come out better for it.

Saying this or something similar puts your focus on the growth that is possible for you from the experience, not the negative aspects, so you can simply handle the situation better. With your focus on how the experience will better you, the Universe affirms and expands that which you focus on and the learning opportunities become apparent much quicker.

Is there an experience in your life that tends to happen, in one form or another, over and over again? If so, what do you focus on when this experience pops up? Can you see how your focus perpetuates the experience? What would happen if you focused on what there is to learn from the experience instead? What is the experience trying to teach you?

The good news is that you don't have to wait for this experience to pop up again. You can look for the learning now. Give it a try. When you do this "inner housecleaning" it's likely that if this experience does crop up again, it will be less intense and dissipate quicker.

The sooner you can get to gratitude for any experience, the better. The sooner you can begin to look for what is available for you to learn, the sooner you will transcend the experience. What about great experiences? Transcend them through gratitude and learning all you can from them. Once a great experience is transcended, an even greater experience awaits.

## Gratitude Practice: Saying Thank You

I mentioned earlier that often times, when people express gratitude by saying "thank you" they are doing it out of habit and are not connected to the experience of gratitude. As an experiment, try practicing saying "thank you" in a more connected and authentic way. It is a simple practice. It takes seconds and can have profound results.

To begin with start by noticing how people react to your saying "thank you." Do your very best to not alter how you would typically say "thank you" to somebody. Take this observation time to notice how you feel when you say "thank you" and how the other person responds. This is simply establishing a baseline, something you can compare to later.

After you have a pretty general idea of how it feels when you say "thank you" for everyday, common courtesies, begin the experiment. Here is how the experiment works. When somebody holds the door or the elevator for you, make eye contact with them before saying "thank you." Consciously bring the feeling of gratitude into your body and allow your words, "thank you," to ride on the experience of gratitude you are consciously choosing to have. Watch how the person responds. Notice how different you feel.

You can even do this more intentionally. Find a good friend (maybe somebody else you know who is reading this book) and take turns doing the experiment on each other. Pick who will be A and who will be B. Person A starts out by tossing off a typical, disconnected thank you. Person A and B recognize how it feels to them. Then, person A consciously brings in the feeling of gratitude, makes eye contact, and allows their "thank you" to ride on the gratitude. Both people notice how that feels. Before discussing the experience, switch and have person B be the one saying "thank you." After both people have been the one to say "thank you," discuss the experience from both perspectives.

It is also a very important part of a gratitude practice to say "thank you" to God / Spirit / the Universe / etc. often.

You can say "thank you" for the same thing many times and in many ways. If somebody stops to help you fix a flat tire, you can certainly express gratitude to that person. You can also express gratitude to Spirit for the synchronicity in having that person just so happen to be driving down the same road as you in the same direction as you at the same time that you needed their help. You can add a "thank you" for yourself, for having noticed the synchronicity and participated in sharing your gratitude.

Thanksgiving is one of the steps in affirmative prayer for a reason. Saying "thank you" to Spirit connects us more powerfully to the giving nature of Spirit. It isn't that God is fickle and will stop paying attention to you if you don't say "thank you" enough. That is a purely human invention. Rather, it's that gratitude and appreciation keep the connection clear.

If a hose gets clogged, the water is not deciding to stop flowing because you didn't say "thank you." The hose is clogged and the water cannot flow as easily. The same holds true with Spirit. If we do not maintain a clear and open connection with Spirit, the flow from Spirit will dwindle. Gratitude is one way we keep that connection clear.

## Gratitude Practice: Gratitude Storm

The Gratitude Storm is a practice I learned from Tony Robbins. I have mentioned the studies that scientifically prove that a little bit of anger suppresses our immune system for a long time. Tony theorized that if anger could suppress our immune system, gratitude could improve it. Certainly, experience has proven that gratitude makes people feel better. In any case, it was this idea that inspired the practice of the Gratitude Storm for Tony.

To begin a Gratitude Storm, first decide how long you want to do it. Five minutes is a great amount of time, but sometimes two might be all you feel you can take in the moment. Once a number of minutes for the Gratitude Storm has been chosen, set a timer. The point of selecting a time is to commit to staying in the Storm so that you don't drop out of it before you really get the benefit. Setting a timer allows you to forget about the time and focus completely on the Storm.

Begin by doing your very best to bring an experience of gratitude into your body. Then, start to name things you are grateful for. It is easiest to start with things that are the closest to you and the most obvious: kids, pets, great weather, whatever is readily present and easy to come up with. With each new thing listed, stack the gratitude for that thing on top of the gratitude you have already named. If I bring forward my feelings of gratitude for my wife, I want to keep that gratitude in my experience while I bring in my gratitude for our cats and stack that gratitude on the gratitude for my wife.

In the amount of time you have selected for your Gratitude Storm, your goal is to bring forward as many experiences of gratitude as you can. Storm them. Make your list as fast and as furiously as you can, just like a powerful thunderstorm, stacking gratitude upon gratitude just like the thunderstorm dumps inch of rain upon inch of rain.

If you find yourself in an upset mood, you can try out a Gratitude Storm and see how your mood changes. When you are happy you can try out a Gratitude Storm and see how much happier you become. You can do a Gratitude Storm at any time when you are in any mood.

Like all practices, it might take a lot more effort at first. In the beginning, you may only bring up ten things in a five minute Storm. No worries. Those ten things will come forward much easier in your next Storm and you will have more time to explore other areas of your life where you find gratitude. The more involved in the Storm you are, the more surprised you might be by what comes forward.

## Gratitude Practice: The "I am grateful for..." Game

This gratitude practice is a slight twist on the "I love..." game from the chapter on Love. In the "I am grateful for..." game you simply look around you for things for which you find gratitude. As an easy place to start, those things that you would select for the "I love..." game are perfect for the "I am grateful for..." game. I am grateful for the beautiful sky. I am grateful for the table, overlooking the ocean, as the perfect place for me to write this chapter. I am grateful for the lovely music playing in the lounge in which I find myself.

The point of this game is to train your awareness to look for things for which you are grateful. The more trained your consciousness is toward gratitude, the more automatically gratitude will come into your experience.

It's also a great idea to play the "I am grateful for..." game when you find yourself in an experience of discord. Whenever things are not how you want them and you're feeling upset, angry, trapped, victimized, or whatever, if you turn to gratitude you will shift your experience out of discord and into harmony.

This will also help to condition your consciousness in a very beneficial way. If, as soon as you notice an experience you are not fond of, you start looking for gratitude, you will train your subconscious mind to use negative experiences as a trigger for gratitude. This training may take a while, but eventually it is possible that without even realizing you are doing it, you will automatically start looking for gratitude as soon as an upset arises.

## Gratitude Practice: Gratitude Journal

A gratitude journal is a blank book dedicated solely to your experiences of gratitude. You want the journal to be specific to your experiences of gratitude. Over time, you will create a resource that you can reference any time you want to experience gratitude. Be as detailed as possible. Describe the experience of gratitude in depth: what happened, how you felt, what you thought about that helped to make the gratitude even richer, etc. This way, when you open the journal to a random page to get an experience of gratitude, you will have an exquisite reminder of your experience. Triggering the memory of the experience will also trigger a fresh batch of gratitude.

You can certainly write in your gratitude journal all throughout the day. However, writing just before bed is an exceptionally beneficial time. If you do not write before bed, reviewing what was written before going to sleep is a wonderful idea.

Have you ever watched a horror movie right before bed and had dreams that felt very similar to the movie? The same could be said for reading a book in which you were exceptionally engaged. We tend to take into our sleep that which is in our awareness right before going to bed. If you finish your day with journaling your gratitude or by reviewing your journal, you will carry that experience of gratitude with you into your sleep and help to anchor gratitude into your consciousness as who you are.

## How Gratitude Helps Bring Complete Emancipation from all Discord of Every Nature

Discord and gratitude can't coexist. There is no discord in an experience of gratitude. By developing your consciousness of gratitude, practicing gratitude and ingraining gratitude into who you are, you emancipate yourself from discord to the degree that you embody gratitude. Even circumstances that would, for most of humanity, be considered full of discord can be free of it if you are able to bring gratitude for the potential growth inherent in the experience to the experience.

Like most spiritual practices, gratitude has a stacking effect. The more you bring gratitude into your experience, the easier it is to experience more gratitude. Gratitude feels good. Feeling good is liberating. It frees up your energy.

To a large degree, the discord you experience is a result of your conditioning. The race consciousness of which we are all a part tends toward discordant thinking. Without your intention, attention, and energy directed toward reconditioning your consciousness to respond to your experiences in a harmonious way, discord will remain. The increased energy that you experience as you bring more gratitude into your life can be applied to that reconditioning of your consciousness toward harmony and away from discord.

Through the application of gratitude to your efforts in manifestation, you will see more powerful results more quickly. This experience can serve to build your faith. The greater your reliance on your faith, through the foundation of your experience, the quicker and easier you will be able to move out of discord and into harmony.

Asking yourself to move into an experience of gratitude when you find yourself faced with difficulty can be asking a lot. It isn't always easy to see the benefit in a situation. It sometimes seems impossible to find any possible benefit at all related to what you're going through. Faith helps you move into that gratitude even when you can't possibly fathom how good could come from what is before you.

As you train yourself to turn to gratitude in experiences of upset, doing so will eventually become automatic. An experience of upset will automatically trigger gratitude which will help to take you right out of the upset and thereby the discordant experience.

The more you practice gratitude, the more spontaneous it will become. Spontaneous gratitude is such an amazing experience. The more you practice gratitude, the more gratitude hunts you down. The more you experience gratitude, the deeper your experiences of gratitude become. The depths of experience available to you in gratitude are limitless. Gratitude can sneak up on you and so fill you that it pours forth from your lips in repeated exclamations of "thank you" and from your eyes as tears of rapturous joy.

I have been fortunate enough to have had a few such experiences as of the writing of this book. On one in particular, I began my day in upset. I don't recall for sure what the trigger of my upset was, but I knew I needed to do something to change my mood, so I started listening to some uplifting music. Eventually a song came on that my wife and I had put on a mix CD that was given out as a favor at our wedding. Suddenly, gratitude tackled me. My heart opened up and I was able to perceive all the love and support in my life. The presence of Spirit as an active force in my life became crystal clear. As the words "thank you God" spilled from my mouth over and over again, joy-filled tears burst forth from my eyes.

This experience and even deeper experiences of gratitude are available to you. But, you must cultivate them. If you are to open to such experiences then you must practice gratitude and become more and more familiar with it. The more you harmonize with gratitude, through your practice, the more of a gratitude magnet you will become.

## Treatment regarding Gratitude

**Recognition:** *There is only one Presence and one Power active as the Universe and as my Life. I call this one Presence and one Power God, Spirit, Life itself. It is whole, complete, and perfect. It is all that there is. There is only this One.*

**Unification:** *I am that which this One is. It is the only thing happening here, or anywhere, and so It must be happening in me, as me, and through me. My nature is the same as Spirit's nature. While Spirit is so much more than what I am, in Truth, all that I am is Spirit.*

**Realization:** *In Spirit is all sufficiency. There is no lack of anything anywhere ever in Spirit. All is provided abundantly, for Spirit is all there is. There can be nothing more than "all there is" so there can be nothing missing. In this I find gratitude. Gratitude. No matter what my experience may be I recognize that I am experiencing it for a reason. There is good to be had in every experience, no matter how difficult it may be to see it initially. I am grateful for this good. I recognize its potential regardless of my ability to see it in the moment and so I bring gratitude into my every experience right from the beginning.*

*My consciousness is a gratitude generating machine! I practice gratitude and in so doing, condition my sub-conscious mind to bring into my awareness that which I am grateful for all the time. Whenever I find myself in upset, my sub-conscious mind instantly presents me with a buffet of gratitude upon which I choose to feast, bringing harmony into my every experience.*

*I am a magnet for gratitude. Gratitude is so attracted to me that it hunts me down no matter where I am. Gratitude could not resist me if it wanted to! Gratitude is my nature. Gratitude is who I am and I experience myself as gratitude regularly and powerfully!*

***Thanksgiving:*** *I am so grateful for gratitude! I appreciate appreciation! Wave after wave of gratitude emanates from my heart, carrying this prayer to manifestation in my life. Thank you, God. Thank you, Spirit. Thank you, Life. Thank you, Gratitude!*

***Release:*** *I release this prayer into the Law of Manifestation, knowing that the gratitude upon which it soars guarantees its manifestation in my life. Knowing that this, or something even better for the Highest Good of all concerned already is, I proclaim this prayer good and very good. It is done. And So It Is!*

# Chapter Sixteen

# Spirtual Practice: Spiritual Education

*"Every now and then a man's mind is stretched by a new idea or sensation, and never shrinks back to its former dimensions."*

~Oliver Wendell Holmes Sr.

*"Once a profound truth has been seen, it cannot be 'unseen'."*

~David Sim

*I*t may seem odd to consider education a spiritual practice and yet, it is a vital component of any spiritual practice. You must learn about spirituality in order to practice spirituality. Spiritual education spurs you forward in your growth and positive change. Spiritual education expands your mind with new ideas. Spiritual education helps you to see profound Truth.

*"You can never solve a problem on the level on which it was created."*

~Albert Einstein

In other words, any problem in your life cannot be addressed at the same level of the problem. You have to learn something new to bring to the problem to transcend it. In relation to your spiritual practice, spiritual education brings you this learning.

Spiritual education also conveys your commitment to the Universe. To a certain extent, many people tend to pay lip service to their dreams and desires. You have probably heard someone talk about all the things they want to experience in their life, yet not take any step toward actually bringing about those experiences. Actions speak louder than words and the Universe hears very clearly. If you say you want something but never commit to having it and never take actions toward creating it, the message the Universe receives is that you don't really want what you say you want and it responds accordingly.

When you engage in spiritual education, you tell the Universe you are serious. Spiritual education requires an investment of your time, attention, and often financial resources. Through engaging in spiritual education you "put your money where your mouth is."

The great news about crafting and engaging in a spiritual practice is that there is always more to learn. There will always be new ideas to consider and new practices to try out. You could learn 100 new things a day relating to spirituality, for 100 years, only to discover how much more there is yet to learn. The Universe is infinite. As such, no matter how much spiritual education you receive, there is an infinite amount more to be had.

I find this endlessly exciting! With all that I have learned, and how miraculously it has improved my life, there is still an infinite amount more that I can learn. And that means an infinite amount more of miraculous improvement and growth? Ooooooo, exciting!

Here is another bit of Einsteinian wisdom for you to chew on...

*"The most incomprehensible thing about the universe is that it is comprehensible."*

In other words, everything ultimately is knowable. The idea that there is an infinity of learning available to you could seem really overwhelming. And yet, in some paradoxical way, according to somebody way smarter than most, it is all knowable. Though there is a limitless amount available to know, it is possible to know any part of it you put your attention on.

## What Counts as Spiritual Education?

The good news about spiritual education is that from the right mindset, just about anything can count as spiritual education. Neil deGrasse Tyson, when pressed for a label, labeled himself agnostic in a video for www.bigthink. com. And yet his video on what he thinks is the most astounding fact about the universe (http://www.youtube. com/watch?v=9D05ej8u-gU) is a phenomenal piece of spiritual education. Or, it can be. Gardening can provide spiritual education. Petting your dog or cat can provide spiritual education. It all comes down to the perspective you bring to the activity you are engaged in.

If, for example, you attend a Sunday church service out of a sense of obligation, but don't want to be there and don't pay attention, then an opportunity for spiritual education has been missed. If you go to the symphony with the intention of allowing the music to teach you something about Spirit, you will not only enjoy the music, but be engaged in spiritual education as well.

It is commonly said that if you want to learn about unconditional love, spend some time with a dog. If your time with the dog is spent upset about having to pick up after it on a walk, your focus will not be attuned to spiritual education. If, on the other hand, you look to the dog to teach you how to be more unconditionally loving, then you are participating in your own spiritual education.

While just about anything can be spiritual education, there are certain things that are much more clearly and obviously fitted in this category.

**Books:** I said earlier that you are already engaged in spiritual education. Reading this book is spiritual education. There is an abundance of spiritually-oriented books. Become a voracious reader. Find as much material to read as you can.

Keep in mind however, just because somebody wrote something down and it got published, does not mean it is necessarily Truth. That includes this book. If something you read does not feel aligned for you, don't take it. If something seems like it might be right, try it on for size. Does it fit? Do you sense that practicing that idea might be helpful? Then practice it. If not, ditch it. There are as many spiritual paths as there are people on the planet. What works for one person, or even millions of people, might not work for you, and that's okay.

**Seminars:** There are also seminars upon seminars to be had, if you like seminars. Sometimes these seminars are with thousands of people and sometimes with just a few. You can find seminars that last for a week or more and some that last for just a few hours. As with books, it is wise to check out everything presented in a seminar before accepting it. There are plenty of ideas that I have learned in seminars that I have rejected as not aligned with me. There are plenty of ideas that I have learned in seminars that I have whole-heartedly accepted and practice to this day.

Something to be aware of with seminars is that, often times, some portion of the seminar will be about offering the participants more seminars, products or services. It is wise to do a little extra research on the seminar leader and check in with your inner guidance before spending large sums of money on products or seminar packages.

**YouTube:** YouTube is full of videos of lectures, keynote speeches, seminars, etc. Find a spiritual teacher you like and search them out on YouTube. You will likely find several videos of various lengths to watch as part of your spiritual education. Often times, the suggested videos on the right side of the screen will link you to teachers you have never heard of before, but who strongly resonate with you. YouTube is a fantastic tool for not only expanding your spiritual education but also for finding new people who inspire you and who teach in a way that you understand.

**Spiritual Counseling:** Some organizations educate and license people as spiritual counselors. I have held a license as a spiritual counselor (called Practitioner) through the Centers for Spiritual Living for many years. Spiritual counseling can help you work through an issue you're facing and provide excellent, hands-on spiritual education.

If you are interested in spiritual counseling, do your research first. If somebody presents themselves as a spiritual counselor, find out about their education. Look into their licensing. Somebody who is not well trained can do more damage than good. However, a professional with good training and experience can be a wonderfully beneficial presence. I, personally, have engaged in spiritual counseling sessions for several years. When I committed to my spiritual growth and education at that level, things began to shift much more quickly and powerfully than they ever did before.

It must be made very, VERY clear that spiritual counseling is NOT therapy. Spiritual counseling may have therapeutic effects but it is not at all the same thing. Do not, under any circumstances, attempt to replace therapy with spiritual counseling. Ever.

**Books on CD / Audio Books:** Many excellent books on spirituality and other related topics have been recorded. Sometimes, seminars are recorded and put out in CD format as well. Libraries have hundreds of hours of spiritual books, seminars, lectures, etc. on CD. As long as you return them on time, it will cost you nothing but your time to go check them out. Time spent on the road makes for excellent listening time. If you are going to be on the road anyway, why not make good use of that time? Checking out these resources is a great way to explore new authors with the only additional investment being the time it takes to check them out.

**Book Clubs / Discussion Groups:** Find like-minded people and hang out with them. "Birds of a feather flock together" is more than just a fun phrase. It is actually a spiritual principle. We tend to gravitate toward people who hold similar ideas and energetic frequencies. There can be a great deal of spiritual education found in sharing ideas and discussing them with other people who are exploring them as well. Different people will read the same sentence differently and achieve different learning based on their experiences. Your thoughts and ideas can expand their thoughts and ideas just like theirs can expand yours.

**Sunday or Midweek Services:** Wait a second!! Isn't this book called *"Church-Free Spirituality"?!* Yes, it is. Church is absolutely not required for a spiritual practice. And yet, a church or a spiritual center can be a great resource for spiritual education. There are many different philosophies that hold regular services. Some are absolutely religion to the core and others teach more spiritual philosophies than religion. The resources section at the end of this book will give you some starting points if you are interested in exploring this option.

As you delve deeper into your spiritual education and progress in your spiritual practice, life will start to provide you with spiritually educational experiences. My original claim that pretty much anything can be spiritual education when you approach it with the mindset of learning about your spirituality holds true, though at first this may not seem to be the case.

For me, I increasingly find more things remind me of my spiritual practice and teach me more about it and myself. A year from now, even more every day experiences will show up as spiritual education for me than do now. It cannot be repeated too much. You can only begin right where you are and allow your practice to grow as you practice.

## How Spiritual Education Helps Bring Complete Emancipation from All Discord of Every Nature

Without spiritual education you will not have spiritual practices that you can engage in on the road to this "complete emancipation." Spiritual education brings new thoughts and new ideas into your awareness. As you learn more about spirituality, your consciousness grows. Through that growth in consciousness you shall come to the place in your life where discord is no longer present.

Because you're reading this book, it's likely that you are interested in yourself as a spiritual being. You're probably interested in spirituality and how to establish it as a foundational piece of your life. Feed that interest. That interest is fed with information and education. Allow the limitless potential you have for learning about yourself and your spirituality to excite you. When you become well versed in educating yourself spiritually, you start to look for the educational opportunities in everything.

While the information for spiritual education can be found in books, CDs, videos, lectures, workshops, etc., it is ultimately up to you to be responsible for your education. The teachers are out there. The resources are available. The only person who can learn for you is you, by your own efforts. Honor your commitment to yourself and your spirituality by learning all you can about it. Show the Universe how serious you are about your own personal learning and growth by diving in deep!

## Treatment regarding Spiritual Education

**Recognition:** *God is all there is. Life is all there is. Spirit is all there is. Oneness is all there is. There is only one Life, one Truth, one Presence, and one Power. This One expresses in each and every individual equally, fully, and completely.*

**Unification:** *As this One expresses equally, fully, and completely in every individual, it expresses equally, fully, and completely in and as me. I Am that I Am.*

**Realization:** *Spirit expresses in, as, and through each individual. As such, Spirit can only express in the world through me to the degree that I understand Its expression as me. Therefore, it logically follows that Spirit is interested and invested in my spiritual education.*

*There is only One. One Spirit. One Life. One Intelligence. Within and as this One, everything is known. The infinitude of what can be known is already known in this One Intelligence that has individuated Itself in me. I have access to this limitless knowing. Everything that is knowable can be known by one and all. It can be known by me.*

*And so I am, like Spirit is, deeply interested in my spiritual education. I invest my time, attention, and resources into my spiritual education in ways that fulfill and uplift me. I reside in the faith that as I commit to my spiritual education, all the resources, information, and teachers show up in exactly the divine, right timing and order. The entire Universe yearns for me to know myself fully and conspires for my Highest Good through my spiritual education.*

*Recognizing that I can learn about myself and my expression of spirituality through every experience, my first response to every situation is to look for the spiritual education opportunity available to me. Trusting in my spiritual practice to show me more about me, I commit to and engage deeply in my spiritual practice, starting right where I am and trusting that my progress along my spiritual path happens in the perfection that is Spirit.*

***Thanksgiving:*** *I am overcome with gratitude for the knowing that Spirit supports and encourages me in my spiritual education. I give thanks to Spirit for all of Its ever-present love and support. I give thanks to myself for my* *willingness to educate myself about spirituality and how I fit into the Spiritual Universe.*

**Release:** *Knowing that all is well, complete, and perfect – for all is God – I release this prayer, allowing it to be. As this prayer manifests through divine spiritual law I know that this prayer or something even better for the Highest Good of all concerned already is. I claim it. I know it. I open to and receive it. And So It Is.*

# Part III

# Chapter Seventeen

## Authority and Responsibility

Responsibility is a big word that can carry quite an emotional charge, yet it is a concept that is important to understand. In this context, responsibility is not meant to convey blame or fault but rather authority. You are the authority in your life. You are the only person who determines what you think, and therefore how you feel, about what happens around you. You even have the authority to give your power away and look to the world or other people to tell you how to think and feel.

Giving your power away is choosing to be a victim. That may sound harsh, but it is absolutely the case. This is so pervasive in society that very few people realize when it's happening, but there are some clues that can help you to recognize when you are giving away your power.

A sudden drop in energy or a feeling of helplessness is a possible indication that you are not consciously choosing what to think and how to feel. Sudden frustration is also likely a symptom of giving away your authority. Feeling like a victim is generally an indication that, to a certain extent, you have given away your power.

When you find yourself in such an experience, it is possible to reclaim your power and authority. First, become as still internally as possible. There is often a lot of internal agitation going on when we give away our authority. Take a deep, conscious breath or two and say to yourself something along the lines of "I reclaim my power. I decide how I think and feel. I am the authority in my life." Visualize your power and authority returning to you in whatever way works best for you. This short intervention or something similar, along with the intention to recall your power, should provide a shift in your experience.

## Authority in Religion and Spirituality

Whether intended or not, most religion comes with an individual's abdication of responsibility to one degree or another. Instead of claiming their own authority in their spiritual progress, people tend to look to church leadership as the gate-keeper. There is even a hierarchy in place through which we give away personal responsibility in varying degrees to varying levels of hierarchy.

Spirituality, on the other hand, has no hierarchy. There is only you and Spirit. This is great news, with a catch. In my spiritual practice, there is only me and Spirit. In your spiritual practice, there is only you and Spirit. You may turn to teachers for spiritual education, but really the dance is between you and God. In that dance, you are the leader. You can take the dance wherever you want to take it. You can include whatever dance steps you choose. Spirit will follow your lead. You have complete freedom in the dance, complete responsibility.

To put it a different way, imagine a giant mansion with 10,000 rooms. This mansion is symbolic of our consciousness or our spiritual practice. There is only one key. It opens every single door in this mansion. You have that key. You can open any door you want to open. In order to do so, you have to get to the door. You have to insert the key and unlock it. You have to open the door. Nobody will do it for you. Teachers and guides may provide you with a map of the mansion, but that is all. That is the catch. I have to do it for myself and you have to do it for yourself.

I can be given countless books on spirituality. I can receive scholarships into 100 seminars. If I never read a page or never actually go to a seminar, it doesn't matter. Nobody can make me learn. Nobody can make me establish a spiritual practice. I have to do that for myself. Nobody can meditate for me. I must make the time for meditation. I can certainly get somebody else to pray for me, but unless I am willing to accept the demonstration of their prayer, it will not matter.

And again, this is good news. The butterfly is responsible for its own emerging from the cocoon, just like we are. What happens if somebody else tries to take responsibility for getting the butterfly out of the cocoon? It may well live but will likely never fly, as the struggle to birth itself from the cocoon provides its wings the strength they need for flight. As much as part of me wishes that Spirit would just do it all for me, and with a metaphorical "snap of Its fingers" suddenly bestow upon me complete enlightenment, I recognize that to do so before I am ready would have disastrous results.

In your life and spiritual practice you have complete authority and responsibility. You can do with that authority and responsibility whatever you wish. You can claim it, take command of your life and direct its course as you choose. You can give it away to the world, to society, to your boss at work, to the stock market, to whatever you want to, and to the degree that you give away your power you will become a victim. This is neither good, nor bad. It just is. You are free and can choose what you will. The truth is, however, the only way to ever reach complete emancipation from discord of every nature is through accepting and claiming your full authority and responsibility.

This is actually a very loving set-up. Nothing is forced on you. You are allowed to choose your own path in your own timing. From the spiritual perspective, everybody is eternal and everybody will arrive at the same place, which is the recognition and experience of ourselves as complete, total, Unconditional Love. As such, it doesn't matter what road you take to get there or how long you linger along the way. Spirit doesn't care. In Spirit, it is already a done deal.

The Bible indicates that we are created in the image and likeness of God. What is forced upon God or Spirit? Nothing. God or Spirit is fully and completely responsible for Itself. So, being born in the image and likeness of God, you too must be completely free and have nothing forced upon you. In setting it up this way, Spirit is doing us a great honor.

Imagine you are having a conversation with Spirit, and Spirit says to you, "I trust you fully and completely. You have full authority and responsibility over yourself, over your life, over your growth, over your experience. I have given you everything you will ever need. You are whole, complete, perfect, and eternal. Nothing you do with this authority and responsibility will ever change that. So, go have fun. Learn everything there is to know about you. The power of creation is yours. Do with it what you will."

Can you imagine a more loving set-up than that? The only way it would be possible for us to be completely free is for us to have complete authority and responsibility. The human race has spent generation after generation giving away that freedom, responsibility, and authority. Humanity has become so good at giving away power that it is far easier, at first, to look outside of ourselves and find people, places, structures, etc. that are eager to gobble up any authority that is set down.

Here is the good news. You never really gave up your authority. You just acted like you did. You can't give up your authority. You can't give up your freedom. You can't give up your responsibility. You can't do this anymore than Spirit could give up Its responsibility, authority, and freedom. What could Spirit give it to? Spirit is all there is. What could you give it to? The dance is just you and Spirit. You can reclaim your authority and responsibility from anything at any time you choose.

There is no special way to reclaim your authority. You just do it. Is there any area in life in which you feel like a victim? Find a simple one. Close your eyes. Intentionally recall your authority from that situation. You can visualize it coming back into your body if that helps. Feel your authority returning to you. Do you feel more empowered, even just a little bit? This takes practice. If you didn't feel any return of freedom or power or authority, no worries. It might take some more practice for you. You may not be able to recall all of your authority at one attempt, and if your habit pattern is to give your authority over, you may have to recall it time and time again. So what? Do it. It will get easier with practice.

# Chapter Eighteen

# Metaphysical Guilt

*M*any times throughout this book I have said that everybody creates their own experience. When your experience is one that you're seeking, it is wonderful to hear that you've created it. But what about when the experience is not what you really want? This is one of the difficulties with the metaphysical philosophy. When experiencing something that is unpleasant, it's easy to fall into what has been called metaphysical guilt, or metaphysical malpractice.

"If I create my experience, and the experience I am having is not what I want to have, then what is wrong with me? I must be doing something wrong! I must be a very bad metaphysician. There is something wrong with my consciousness or else I wouldn't be having this experience." All of these statements are examples of metaphysical guilt. I strongly urge you in your spiritual practice to keep a watchful ear out for such thoughts. They are not helpful and they are not kind.

Metaphysical malpractice arrests your forward progress through the very spiritual laws that you are utilizing to grow. If in one moment you say "I am so grateful to have manifested this great new job," and in the next "but I still don't have the perfect relationship so something must be wrong with me and my consciousness," you have taken one step forward and one step back.

While it is common in some circles for others to insinuate that something is wrong with your consciousness when you're experiencing this dilemma, the primary source of metaphysical malpractice is our own self talk. Careful! "I am the biggest source of my metaphysical guilt, something is wrong with me," is just around the corner. Don't go there.

Let's put a little perspective on the habit of metaphysical malpractice. Why would anybody choose to think such thoughts? The answer might be surprising. Metaphysical malpractice is a preservation mechanism. That's right. The intent behind metaphysical guilt is to keep you safe and alive. How is this so?

As you engage in a spiritual practice you begin to rise above race consciousness. You cease to operate on default and begin to operate from a place of greater conscious choice. That portion of your consciousness that is in charge of keeping you alive and safe, the "ego," freaks out when you grow spiritually.

Whether or not you're thriving in your life or just barely scraping by, the part of you that needs to keep you alive says, "I am alive. Period. I am alive and that means what I am doing is working." From this perspective when you change how you operate, you are moving into the unknown. To that piece of yourself that keeps you alive in the world, the unknown means death.

So you see, on a lower level of awareness, metaphysical guilt is a mechanism of self-preservation. It is not bad. It is not wrong. Its intention is to keep you safe and alive. This is a wonderful thing when you're in danger but in the context of metaphysical guilt it is out of place. And, because you create your experience, it is your responsibility to keep yourself as free from it as possible.

## Keeping Free of Self-Imposed
## Metaphysical Malpractice / Guilt

First and foremost, you must be aware of when you are engaging in metaphysical malpractice. This is done purely through attention and intention. Set the intention within yourself to notice quickly whenever you're using spirituality to produce guilty feelings. At first, you may not be aware that you are engaging in metaphysical guilt at all. After setting the intention to catch yourself, you will notice on occasion. The more you notice, the more you will notice. It may even get to the point where it feels like you're catching yourself in metaphysical guilt all the time. Eventually, you will start noticing less and less because your awareness has caused the habit to decrease in frequency.

Once you do notice you are guilting yourself out of your forward progress, there are a few things you can do to help stop the thoughts. First and foremost is to thank that part of yourself that is doing the metaphysical guilt for being so vigilant in keeping you safe. Remember, it's doing what it is supposed to do; it's just out of context. Then, give yourself the appropriate context. It might go something like this, "Thank you for helping to keep me safe. In this instance, however, there is no danger. This is good and safe and will bring even more life than I had before." Use whatever words that work for you. Am I advising talking to yourself? Yes! Absolutely! Just be aware of doing so out loud around other people, as they might get the wrong idea!

Another way of handling metaphysical guilt is to use it for your benefit. "What is wrong with my consciousness that I am having this experience?" "Well, nothing is wrong. It is what it is. And, now that I have noticed what is going on, what am I believing about myself or this situation that is making my experience what it is? What could I believe differently that would change my experience?" Using both of these options in conjunction will turn what used to be a detriment to your growth into a spring board.

## Keeping Free of Metaphysical Malpractice / Guilt from Others

When it comes to statements of metaphysical guilt directed at you from others, you have another dimension to deal with. First and foremost, it is very important to be solid in the understanding and awareness that somebody directing metaphysical malpractice toward you has NOTHING to do with you. You do not have to take it on. If people say "Well, you know you are causing that, so it looks like you have some work to do," it is riding on their judgment of their spiritual practice, not yours. They are choosing to see in your practice what they dislike about theirs and putting it on you is easier than dealing with it themselves.

Once you are clear on this, your next step is to remove yourself from the situation. This can be done by exiting the conversation, politely changing the subject or even saying, "Thank you for sharing. I'll look into that." Do not engage with the energy of metaphysical guilt on any level if you can help it.

Finally, it can only benefit you to actually check out what was said. You will either find that there is no factual basis for it and be done with it, or discover a thought or belief that you could update. Either way, you are benefited.

## Metaphysical Guilt Related to Health

Health is one of the areas of our lives that is the most ripe for metaphysical guilt. I have personally struggled with this significantly. In the not so distant past, a cold would become a spiritual crisis. "How can I claim to be somebody with the authority to write and speak about spirituality while I have a cold? If I say 'you create your experience' then am I not creating this cold? I must not be good enough to prevent something so simple as a cold. Who do I think I am?" Such thoughts tend to come from a belief in unworthiness, which the majority of humanity deals with to one degree or another.

In working through metaphysical guilt, no matter what it might be related to, the first step is noticing what is happening and the second is being thankful. The guilt is there to keep you safe. In this case, there is no need for it to keep me safe. Now I can look at what I believe about myself and the situation and change the beliefs and thoughts that are not serving me by choosing more empowering beliefs.

The question "Do we create our health issues?" often comes up in this arena. The more significant the health challenge, the weightier this question becomes. Does the person with asthma or cancer create their asthma or cancer? My answer to this question is simply that it does not matter. If there are no clear environmental causes (like living next to a coal mine and having breathing difficulty) that can be eliminated, it doesn't matter how a significant health challenge came to be in a person's experience. What matters is that it is part of their experience and, with their attitude and spiritual practice, they can influence their experience related to the health challenge. You can expend energy wondering and worrying about if you caused a health condition or not, or, you can direct your energy toward returning to health. One choice is energy well spent and the other is energy wasted.

A few books that I have found very helpful relating to health challenges and spirituality are listed in the Resources section at the end of the book.

# Chapter Nineteen

## Community

The premise of *Church-Free Spirituality* is that spirituality can be completely separate from religion. You can have a fulfilling spiritual practice within a religion if you like. You can also have a fulfilling spiritual practice without religion. There is no requirement to join any particular belief system or subscribe to any certain philosophy. It is completely possible to do your spiritual journey totally on your own if you so choose. As a perfect expression of Spirit (we all are that) you have access to the infinite knowingness of Spirit, just like everybody does. However, the support, encouragement, and learning available as part of a spiritual community can be exceptionally beneficial in your spiritual practice. I encourage seeking one out if and when it feels appropriate.

### Birds of a Feather Flock Together

As you progress you may well find that your spiritual community is forming around you. "Birds of a feather flock together" and "like attracts like." As you harmonize to a different vibration through your spiritual practice, some of the people in your life may become dissonant with your vibration and show up in your experience less and less. At the same time, you will likely meet new people who are more harmonized with the vibration you are creating and possibly form very beneficial relationships with them.

This is an important point to really get deeply. As you grow you will need to be willing to let go of relationships that no longer serve you. This is not mean-spirited and it is not at all a judgment of anybody or their process.

There are many people that I used to spend significant amounts of time with in my life that I no longer communicate with at all. I still love them. I still bless them and want the very best for them in their lives. It is just that the vibration they are holding and the vibration that I am holding do not harmonize like they used to.

This doesn't mean I am better than they are by any means. Direct sun light, of itself, is not any better or worse than indirect sun light. Yet some plants flourish with indirect sun while others will wither, and vice versa.

How will you know if it is time to adjust how and with whom you spend your time? Simply notice how your body feels. The human body is a phenomenally precise measurement instrument. The more you tune into yours, the better you will get at reading it and understanding what it is telling you.

If you find that spending time with a certain person or doing a certain activity leaves you feeling really drained, perhaps it would be a good idea to spend less time in that way. If you pay attention, you will start to notice when something "feels off." Explore those feelings deeply. It may be that the "off" feelings are indicating that the new vibration you are creating is becoming discordant with the energy of the particular person or experience.

When this starts to happen it can be difficult, especially if the person has been in your life for a long time. What can you do if you notice this starting to happen? You could share with this person about your spiritual practice. They may be interested in establishing one as well. If they begin to focus on the spiritual side of life, it is possible that their vibrational shift from engaging in their own spiritual practice will re-harmonize them with you. This is not something that can be forced. In fact, the forcing energy will likely only perpetuate the dissonance.

Primarily though, the "thing to do" is to do your very best with releasing your attachment to the relationship and allow it to take its course, whatever that may be. If the relationship fades, it does not mean that you don't care about the person anymore. I still think, from time to time, about those friends who are no longer a part of my life and send them my love. I love them. I bless them. I don't spend my time with them.

## Spiritual Communities

When trying to figure out which spiritual community is right for you, un-limit yourself. Society typically places churches as the only sort of community available as related to spirituality, but there are many other options. If a church works for you, great! *Church-Free Spirituality* doesn't mean you can't go to a church if you want to, it just means that your spirituality and your church are not necessarily coupled.

There are also spiritual centers that function like churches. If you enjoy the church feel, but not what churches teach, these spiritual organizations may be great for you. The two primary spiritually focused, church-like organizations that I am aware of are Unity and Centers for Spiritual Living (formerly Religious Science, which is *NOT* Scientology). I was raised in Unity and have and also spent significant time with Centers for Spiritual Living.

There are study groups or book clubs. These tend to be less formally organized than the church-like spiritual organizations, but can be wonderful sources of community. Some may have more formalized leaders and some might just be groups of peers that read a spiritually focused book together and discuss what it means to them. This discussion can help the other members of the group to get more out of a book than they otherwise would have. When I hear how somebody else understands an idea, it expands my awareness. The very act of sharing my understanding with others causes me to explore my understanding and deepen it.

Mastermind groups are also wonderful. A Mastermind group is a small group of people who get together regularly to support each other in whatever it is they are working on in their lives. There are sure to be Mastermind groups related to spirituality and some that are generic, with no specific purpose but the general supportive structure for whatever members are seeking to achieve.

Engaging in spiritual community helps to grease the wheels, so to speak. You learn from those around you and they learn from you. The energy of the group also supports you in growing as fully, robustly, and quickly as possible. Science has proven that everything is energy and that we create and are affected by energy fields. A group of people, committed to spiritual growth, pool their intentions when they get together. The energy of those combined intentions will benefit you and the entire group.

## You Are the Only Authority You Need

Let's speak frankly for a moment about the potential dangers of groups that claim to be spiritual but are just masquerading. I hesitate to use the word "cult" because the actual definition of a cult is far different than how it is commonly used. There are many definitions of the word "cult" and most of them do not have negative connotations, such as "great devotion to a person, idea, object, movement or work." (www.merriam-webster.com/dictionary/cult). That definition clearly includes spirituality. I have great devotion to the ideas of spirituality and the movement of spirituality expanding throughout the world. Often times, philosophies or belief systems that don't adhere to traditional religious beliefs are labeled as "cults."

The dangerous "cults" tend to be quite different. Beware of any group that demands you give up your individuality to the group. Beware of any group whose leader places him or herself as better than the group members. In authentically spiritual groups, the leader of the group is part of the group and learns from the group as well. The leaders recognize that while they may be farther on the path than some members of the group, they are still on a similar path and are not better than any other person because of where they are in their spiritual progress.

You are the only authority you will ever need. Do not abdicate that authority to anybody. If learning from a particular teacher or group requires you to denigrate yourself, run the other way. You are a perfect, individual expression of Spirit. That which beats your heart is the same energy that has caused the heart of any and every enlightened spiritual master to beat.

This doesn't mean you have nothing to learn – quite the contrary. We all have limitless learning ahead of us. What it means is that you have within you the inherent wisdom to know if a group is right for you or wrong for you. You have the intuitive capacity to tell if a spiritual practice is aligned with Truth or not. Trust it. Check everything out. Do not take anything at face value. If something about a group feels wrong, explore why it feels wrong – from outside of the group. Is it resistance to growth or is it your intuitive capacity telling you that this particular group is NOT for your highest good?

Trust your intuitive capacity and always err on the side of caution. If you don't stick with a group because you think your intuition is telling you it is not your group, but it is really just your resistance to growth, no big deal. You will find another group that will be just as good. If you misinterpret an intuitive warning about a group for resistance to growth, you will have a wealth of learning and growth opportunities that you could have otherwise avoided.

Don't let this little discussion keep you away from exploring spiritual communities. The vast majority of them are just fine. And, if there really is nothing for you to gain from participating in a group that is other than fine, you will naturally steer clear of it or your intuition about the group will be clear.

Finding a spiritual community when the time is right will be of great benefit to you and your spiritual practice. Without my spiritual community and all that I learned there, my life would be significantly different. Through my spiritual community I have a chance to connect to like-minded people. I get to learn and receive support from my community. I get to be of service to my community. It enriches my life and my spiritual practice and has been a wonderful example for me of Spirit showing up in exactly the way that I need. A spiritual community can be that for you as well.

# Chapter Twenty

## Closing Thoughts

First and foremost, I want to thank you. Not for purchasing this book (though I am grateful for that too), but for just being willing to explore the possibility of bringing spirituality more into your life. I have said many times that we are all one and that everything is connected. By choosing to explore your own spirituality, you add to the race consciousness your focus on spirituality. Every time anybody adds any amount of spiritual awareness to humanity's consciousness, it makes it easier for all of us – even those who couldn't care less about spirituality.

The importance of this work cannot be overstated. Those who are truly committed to their spiritual practice find that there is no greater return on investment. One new idea can change a life. One perspective shift can turn a curse into a blessing. I can't fathom what my life would be like today if I hadn't found my way back to my spiritual practice. It took me a lot of work, a lot of time and dedication, but it was all so very worth it. The life I live today is greater by far than my greatest imaginings of what was possible for me ten years ago. There is no more important work that one can do than to work on discovering themselves. And, it is work that is never finished.

I am so very excited by the never-ending nature of spirituality. We have a limitless capacity to love. We have a limitless capacity to experience joy, bliss, peace, and gratitude. The richest person on the planet has not even scratched the surface of wealth, abundance, and prosperity. Our wildest dreams are paltry things when compared to what the Universe has in store for us. Every time one of our wildest dreams becomes our reality, our dreams get even wilder and still they don't come close.

A spiritual practice can radically change your life, but it will take dedication and perseverance. The spiritual path is very rewarding and can be very difficult. Find support. *Church-Free Spirituality* does not necessarily mean solitary spirituality. Look for teachers that you resonate with and learn from them all that you can. Whether or not you are easily able to find the support you need along your spiritual journey, the Universe is always supporting you. Rely on Spirit. It is an inexhaustible source of support.

Trust yourself. Trust your inner guidance. Try out everything this book has to offer. Use what works for you and have the sense and self-confidence to either adjust what doesn't seem to be working, or drop it all together. Your spiritual path is uniquely your own. Many people walk very similar paths, but in the end you are you and your spiritual path is as unique as you are. Seek out spiritual practices not listed in this book as well. This book is a starting place, not an exhaustive list. There are many, many more items on the "spiritual practices menu." Order what you think you might like and send back what you don't.

For those who dedicate themselves to a life-long spiritual practice, there is more richness of experience to be had than can possibly be imagined. I say this from experience. The quality of life that I enjoy today was nowhere close to possible ten years ago, and it is all due to my spiritual practice. I walk this path every day. Some days, I soar. Some days, I stumble, a lot... However, no matter what happens in my walk, I know that Spirit walks every step with me. The same is true for you.

You have read many affirmative prayers throughout this book. I would like to leave you with one more. This affirmative prayer was the first part of this book that was written. It remained on page one of the manuscript until now, at the conclusion of the writing. This affirmative prayer guided the writing of this book.

> *There is only One Life.*
> *This Life is Perfect.*
> *This Life is the Perfect Life of Spirit and It is my Life.*
> *It is the One Life that writes these words and the One Life that reads these words.*
> *As such, any expression of the One reading these words will find benefit.*
> *By the reading of these words, the reader is blessed and sped along their path Home.*
> *In, as, and through the One Life as All, there can be nothing other, save something even better for the Highest Good of All.*
> *And So It Is!*

Thank you. Bless you. I love you.


Ben

# Resources

I have had firsthand experience of everything listed in this section. This list is not the least bit exhaustive. There are many more resources out there available to you.

## Spiritual Centers / Organizations / Spiritual Education

### Unity
www.unity.org

Unity is one of the two primary metaphysical, new thought philosophies at work in the world currently. It leans more toward the Bible and Jesus than the other primary philosophy. Unity centers operate like churches and are often referred to as churches.

### Centers for Spiritual Living (CSL)
www.csl.org

Centers for Spiritual Living (formerly Science of Mind and Religious Science) is the other primary metaphysical, new thought philosophy at work in the world. Their teachings are less Jesus-based than Unity, but still incorporate metaphysical interpretations of the Bible in their philosophy. Centers for Spiritual Living operate like churches.

### Church of the Movement of Spiritual Inner Awareness (MSIA)
www.msia.org

MSIA is very similar to new thought metaphysics but is a little more Eastern based in its philosophy and more esoteric than Unity or CSL. Despite having the word "Church" in its name, MSIA does not function like a church.

Most of its teachings are offered through correspondence courses, books, and workshops.

### University of Santa Monica (USM)
www.universityofsantamonica.edu
USM is a private university in Santa Monica, CA teaching Spiritual Psychology. They offer in-person programs as well as online courses. They do an excellent job of teaching through experience and practice. Their curriculum does a great job of making spirituality very secular.

## Meditation Resources

### Prem Rawat
http://www.wopg.org
Prem Rawat is a meditation teacher from India. I learned his unique meditation technique many years ago. While it did not harmonize with me enough for me to practice it, I do believe that what he teaches is valuable.

### Shambhala
http://www.shambhala.org
Shambhala is a Buddhist philosophy. They have centers in many places that teach walking and sitting meditation techniques. While my personal meditation is not the meditation they teach, I did receive meditation instruction from them and, again, believe that what they teach is valuable.

### *Journey of Awakening* by: Ram Dass
*Journey of Awakening* is a wonderful book on meditation. It is filled with easy practice exercises and does a phenomenal job of discussing meditation.

## Transcendental Meditation®
www.tm.org

Transcendental Meditation, or TM, was brought to the United States from India by Maharishi Mahesh Yogi. It is the most scientifically studied form of meditation with over 350 peer-reviewed research studies having been published. There is a fee to be taught TM, however their ongoing support is top-notch.

## Specific Books

### *It's So Easy When You Know How* by: Rev. Dr. Harry Morgan Moses

This book offers an exquisite overview of spirituality, how to apply it in your life, and its benefits.

### *Quantum Healing* by: Deepak Chopra

*Quantum Healing* is an excellent book about healing as related to spirituality. Its primary focus is on cancer and includes several case studies. While its main focus is on cancer, the ideas presented in this book can be applied to health in general as well.

### *The Third Appearance* by: Walter Starcke

This book does a wonderful job of combining spirituality and science through a mystical awareness.

### *Living the Science of Mind* by: Ernest Holmes

*Living the Science of Mind* is a practical application guide to the philosophy taught through Centers for Spiritual Living.

### *Loyalty to Your Soul* by: Drs. Ron and Mary Hulnick

Drs. Ron and Mary Hulnick founded the University

of Santa Monica. This book is a wonderful introduction to spiritual psychology, taught through USM.

## Authors

In general the authors listed here have wonderfully written books on spirituality. While I have not read everything they have ever written, their works that I have read have all been exceptional.

### Ernest Holmes

Ernest Holmes is the founder of Centers for Spiritual Living. He has written many books on spirituality that range from simple and practical, to exceptionally deep and complex. His books were written a while ago so the language is somewhat outdated, but easy enough to translate in the moment. I highly recommend reading a lot of Ernest Holmes.

### Charles and/or Myrtle Fillmore

Charles and Myrtle Fillmore founded Unity. As with Ernest Holmes, the writing is somewhat dated, but the information is timeless.

### Dr. Wayne Dyer

Dr. Dyer has written prolifically over his career and his books offer excellent insights into spirituality.

### Anthony Robbins

While Tony's work is generally presented in the context of personal empowerment and business, it is sneakily spiritual. He has authored several books, though he is primarily a seminar leader. His work might not come across as spiritual, but from my perspective he teaches a lot

of spiritual principles without calling them out as such. Far
beyond just books, many videos of his seminars can be found
on YouTube.

### Hafiz and Rumi

Rumi and Hafiz are ecstatic poets who lived roughly in
the 1200s and 1300s respectively. The translations of their
poems are beautiful, moving, and overflowing with spiritual
devotion.

28360504R00162

Made in the USA
Columbia, SC
10 October 2018